THE GREAT COOKS' GUIDE TO

Crêpes
& Soufflés

America's leading food authorities share their home-tested recipes and expertise on cooking equipment and techniques

THE GREAT COOKS' GUIDE TO

Crêpes
& Soufflés

A BEARD GLASER WOLF BOOK

RANDOM HOUSE   NEW YORK

Book Design by Milton Glaser, Inc.

Cover Photograph by Richard Jeffery

Library of Congress Cataloguing in Publication Data

Main entry under title:

The Great cooks' guide to crêpes & soufflés.

(The Great cooks' library)
1.   Pancakes, waffles, etc.   2.   Soufflés.   I.   Title: Crêpes & soufflés.   II.   Series.
TX770.G73   641.8   77–5972

ISBN: 394-73422-X
Manufactured in the United States of America
4 6 8 9 7 5 3

We have gathered together some of the great cooks in this country to share their recipes—and their expertise—with you. As you read the recipes, you will find that in certain cases techniques will vary. This is as it should be: cooking is a highly individual art, and our experts have arrived at their own personal methods through years of experience in the kitchen.

THE EDITORS

Contents

SWEET HOT SOUFFLÉS

SWEET COLD SOUFFLÉS

Crêpes

The thin pancake known as a crêpe is far easier than pie to make, yet legions of people assume that a food known by its French name must be difficult to cook. The mystique attached to French cuisine is so powerful that merely seeing French words causes many a splendid cook to suffer an anxiety attack. For example, take *tartine beurrée*. Sounds impressive, doesn't it? Probably beyond the scope of non-professionals. Translate the phrase, though, and you'll find that *tartine beurrée* means—a slice of buttered bread.

If you can forgive the crêpe its fancy name, you'll also find it's not much more trouble to assemble than a *tartine*. Crêpes are really much simpler than American flapjacks—just about as simple as food can be. They consist of eggs, flour, liquid (usually milk) and oil or butter. (For dessert crêpes, sugar is often added; but it's not vital.) Almost every country or culture has its version of the crêpe: in Italy, it's the *crespella*, in Hungary, the *palacsinta*, in Russia, the *blini*, and in Jewish cooking, the *blintz*. Just about everyone but the Eskimos makes some variation of handy flat pancakes. And if everyone does it, crêpe-making can't be so difficult!

The marvelous fact about crêpes is that they are perfect cook-ahead food. They'll keep in the refrigerator (separated by squares of waxed paper and wrapped in plastic) for two days; frozen in batches of six and wrapped airtight, they'll keep for two months. Frozen crêpes will thaw in ten minutes or so, placed in a covered dish in a 300-degree oven. Then they're ready to be filled, sauced, heated if called for, and served. Best of all, you cook crêpes when you want, at *your* leisure, with no one breathing over your shoulder.

Crêpes can't really be praised enough. These lacy, pliable little rounds are inexpensive yet elegant, easy to make and impressive to serve, and delicate but durable. They can be appetizer, main course, or dessert. They are economical, nutritious, and beg to be used with leftovers. Sophisticated diners love them, and so do kids.

Crêpe Pans: To make a crêpe that's thin and delicate, you must have a good pan. It must be heavy enough to distribute the heat evenly, but light enough to handle with ease. The choice may seem bewildering, but any well-made crêpe pan will do the job. Picking a pan is a matter of individual choice. There are essentially two kinds of crêpe-cookers (a third type of crêpe pan, called a finishing pan, we'll describe later). The first is the con-

Iron Crêpe Pan. Heavy iron crêpe pans, the most common type of all, are available in a wide range of sizes from 5″ to 9″ or more across the bottom. For best results, if not employed frequently, they should be seasoned with salt and oil before each use.

Cast-Aluminum Crêpe Pan. Aluminum is an excellent conductor of heat, and when it is as thick as this pan, it holds and distributes heat extremely well. Once seasoned, the pan needs only to be wiped with a paper towel and a little cooking oil to keep it clean. The handsome walnut handle remains cool to the touch.

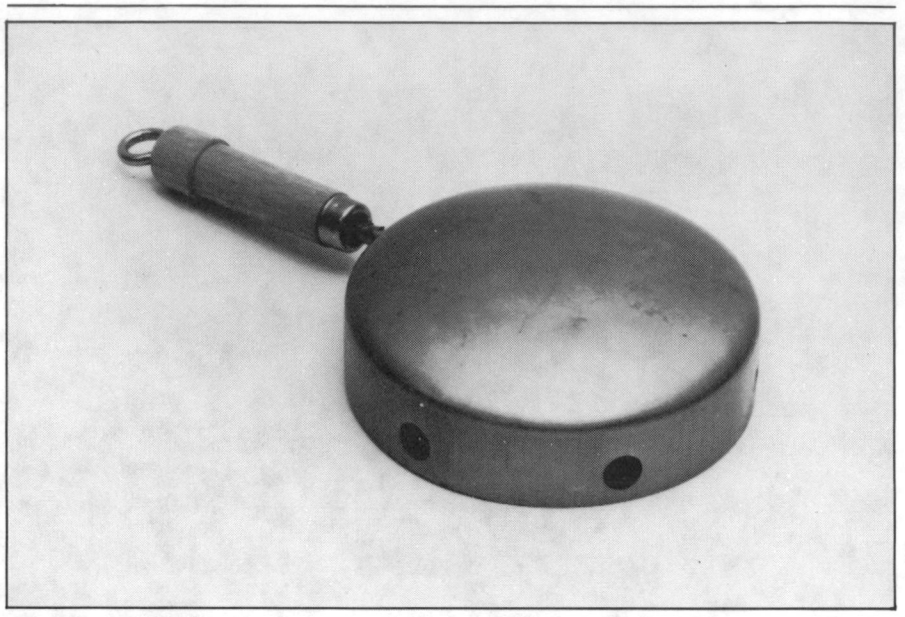

Steel Bottom-Dip Crêpe Pan. Crêpes made on the bottom of a pan are uniform in shape and thickness, and are usually about 7″ to 8″ in diameter. A pan used (on a gas stove) must be perforated like this one to avoid suffocating the flame.

Electric Bottom-Dip Crêpe Pan. Beautifully even, thin crêpes can be made on a bottoms-up pan without the fuss of measuring, if the pan is preheated before it is dipped into the batter. Thermostatically-controlled electricity and a non-stick cooking surface also make for perfect crêpes.

ventional skillet type: in this category are the classic iron or steel pans, unpretentious but sturdy, which turn out 5-inch crêpes. One splendid cast-aluminum pan has the advantage of a walnut-covered handle so it can be used without a potholder. There are copper and stainless pans, and electric ones. Heavy-duty skillets with non-stick interiors make excellent crêpe pans, and can be used for other purposes as well. (In general, most cooks prefer to keep the crêpe pan for crêpes alone. Once they've established a relationship with a very special pan, they won't risk trouble by introducing other foods.) In these pans, batter is swirled around in the heated interior.

Recently a vogue has sprung up for making crêpes on the bottom of pans. The pan is first heated, then dipped in a bowl of batter, then inverted over a flame or heating element. Specially made models come on the market every day; some of them are electrified.

Crêpe-making Accessories: When you've chosen a crêpe pan, follow the manufacturer's directions for seasoning or preparation, if any is required. Then, practice with the pan. The better we know our equipment, the more useful it becomes. Think of the first batch of batter as expendable learning equipment; artists use up paper and paint while they develop their craft, don't they? If your first attempts are edible, so much the better, but the purpose of this trial run is really to become familiar with the ins and outs of your crêpe cooker. First, assemble what you'll need: a shallow bowl of batter for the bottom-dip method, a ladle or small pitcher for the usual method. Have oil or melted butter and a pastry brush, and a sheaf of waxed paper squares to place between finished crêpes on a stacking plate. As you practice, you'll pick up speed.

Cooking Crêpes: The key to successful crêpes is the heat of the pan. It's impossible to make an arbitrary rule—pans differ, and so does the space between heating element and cooking surface. Gas range or electric? That makes a difference, too. Use the water test to see if the heat is right. Flick a few drops onto the heated pan. If the drops steam, the pan's too cold. If they vaporize immediately, it's too hot. When the drops bounce and dance about, the heat is just right.

Most conventional pans take about two tablespoons of batter. (You'll soon find out if this is the right amount.) Grasp the handle and pour batter into the center of the pan. Lift the pan up, swirling the batter around to cover the bottom in a thin layer. Speed is necessary here so that the batter spreads evenly before setting. Return to the heat and cook until the bottom is brown; not uniformly brown like a flapjack, but speckled brown and white. (Pry up an edge with a spatula or fork, and peek.) Brown the other side or not—experts vary on the necessity of this, but most crêpes are turned. (It will never brown as much as the first side.) Slide the crêpe onto the stacking plate and cover it with waxed paper. If you use an upside-down pan, follow the manufacturer's directions. They are quite complete. With any method, the first crêpe or two is soggy, crisp, patchy and/or funny-looking. The French, with a Gallic shrug, dub these failures "pour du beurre"—they're "for the butter."

Copper Presentation Pan. Although it requires more care in cleaning, a copper pan is the most beautiful for tableside finishing. This stainless-steel-lined pan has an aluminum core for even heat distribution.

Should the batter rest, or may it be used at once? An overbeaten batter—one made in a blender or food processor—does need to sit at least an hour at room temperature or to spend a night in the refrigerator. That's because beating toughens a component of flour called gluten. If the batter is allowed to sit, the gluten literally relaxes, and the result is a light and tender crêpe. If you must use a batter right away, make the crêpes by hand, or use the instant-blending brand of flour where the gluten has been knocked to its knees. Batters that sit will thicken; dilute them with a little water to the consistency of heavy cream.

Roll crêpes so that the best side—the one cooked first—shows; fill them and shape them into cigars, fold-overs, pocketfolds, triangles, or cornucopias. In general, it's wisest not to freeze filled crêpes, especially if the sauce is somewhat runny. However, dessert crêpes using whipped cream fillings freeze well. Freeze on cookie sheets, separated, and thaw in the refrigerator before serving.

For the performing cook who likes to flambé food in front of company, there are finishing pans. These are large, flat, beautiful and expensive. One of these finishers would be perfect for both flamed crêpes or the non-flamed, completely fool-proof *crêpes Suzette* appearing in this guide.

Soufflés

Soufflés, like balloons and political rhetoric, rise on hot air. And since what goes up must come down, the soufflé has only a short period of glory. Unlike the patient crêpe that waits until it's needed, the soufflé demands instant attention. *When the soufflé is ready, serve it!* Dessert soufflés go in the oven as the main course is served. Even if everyone has to wait a few extra moments.

Most food is forgiving. It stands up to certain amounts of mishandling, over- and under-cooking, and like Queen Victoria, it *wants* to be good. Soufflés are no different. True, the ideal soufflé is high and light, and holds its breath until it comes to the table. But if the soufflé collapses, or even fails to rise very much, you're left with a tasty pudding. If the worst does happen, treat your fallen soufflé as a *timbale* (a steamed pudding akin to the soufflé but much denser in texture) and just spoon it on to individual plates in the kitchen. If you know that whatever you turn out will be eminently edible, you'll cook with a light heart and hand, and achieve a proper soufflé. However, understanding the mechanics that cause the soufflé to rise will help eliminate failure almost every time.

Equipment: To make a soufflé, you'll need a balloon whisk, rotary beater or electric mixer. Also a large bowl for whipping the egg whites: stainless-steel, glass or ceramic is fine, but plastic is not good. The copper bowl so touted by experts is fine if you want to use it. Copper has a slight chemical reaction with egg whites that helps them to swell and rise, but the same result can be achieved with a pinch of cream of tartar. Other necessary equipment is a small bowl to hold the yolks until they are incorporated into the soufflé base, a saucepan for cooking the base, and a rubber scraper for folding in the egg whites.

To rise properly, soufflés need flat-bottomed, straight-sided containers. The most useful is the 1½-quart size, though 1- and 2-quart molds are often called for, as are the individual small molds. Two quarts is the largest size that should be used—any bigger and the soufflé will cook unevenly. (If you're feeding a crowd, make two soufflés and add five minutes to the cooking time.) Molds come in plain and marvelously decorated porcelain, metal shapes called charlottes, stoneware and glass. (If using glass, remember to reduce the heat by 10 degrees.) You'll also want a baking sheet, preheated in the oven to sit under the soufflé as it cooks, assuring that both top and bottom cook at the same pace. Whatever container you use, don't fill it more than three-quarters full.

Cooking a Soufflé: The basic soufflé consists of a cooked base enriched with egg yolks lightened by stiffly beaten egg whites. (Professionals usually add one extra white for every four whole eggs used.) Well-beaten whites mount to seven times their original volume. One expert insists that they rise higher when at room temperature. At any rate, the bowl must be scrupulously clean, absolutely dry, and contain *not a speck* of yolk or oil of any kind. Any of these will spell disaster. When separating eggs, break them one at a time over a small bowl. Then tip each white into the larger bowl you'll use for beating them. That way, if the yolk should break, the mass of egg white is not contaminated.

The phrase "stiffly beaten whites" can be confusing. At the perfect point they are still glistening, but will not budge when the bowl is tipped and will stand firmly on a beater held upside down (over the bowl!). The whites are folded into the base, which must be cooled to room temperature; heat would collapse the air bubbles you've worked so hard to trap. (Incidentally, you can make the base hours in advance of cooking and store it in the refrigerator. Just bring it to room temperature before folding in the whites.) To fold the whites into the base: add one-third of the whites to the base, whipping them in vigorously with a wire whisk. This lightens the mass so that it won't crush the rest of the whites. With a rubber scraper, scoop the remaining whites on top of the base. Cut down with the spatula from the center to the bottom of the bowl, then draw it up again against the side of the bowl. This demands a delicate touch, but if you keep in mind that you are trying to incorporate base and whites without losing volume, you'll quickly get the hang of it. It's better to leave a few patches of white unblended rather than risk a flat soufflé.

You can, like many professional chefs, chill the prepared soufflé dish for at least half an hour before filling and cooking. They claim that chilling helps a soufflé to rise quickly and straight up. Pop the soufflé into the middle of the oven on the heated baking sheet. Some like their soufflés quite firm, but if you want a creamy center, cook for five minutes less than the recipe calls for. Test by giving the soufflé a gentle shake; the top should shiver slightly.

Cold Soufflés: With a spectacular cold soufflé, you run no risk of surprise. They won't fall and they can be served at your convenience. Cold dessert soufflés are not baked; most of them owe their buoyancy to gelatin, not heat. When mixed with beaten egg whites (and usually whipped cream as well) the gelatin traps the air bubbles and holds them in suspension.

A cold soufflé is most spectacular rising above the rim of its dish. To make sure it does, help it along with a collar of foil, waxed or parchment paper. Cut a strip about eight inches wide and long enough to circle one and one-half times around the rim of the soufflé dish. Fold the strip in half. Butter or oil and sugar it and follow the directions given in the recipe for preparing the mold—in effect, the collar is acting as an extension of the mold. Tie it in place with string. When the collar is removed (just before serving), several impressive inches of soufflé will be left towering above the rim of the dish. Delicate and light, cold soufflés are a perfect ending for an important dinner party.

Porcelain Soufflé Dish. For both cooking and serving, nothing becomes a soufflé more than a heatproof, porcelain dish with a flat bottom and straight, traditionally fluted, sides. This one is ½" deeper than most, good for soufflés with hidden surprises, like lobster meat.

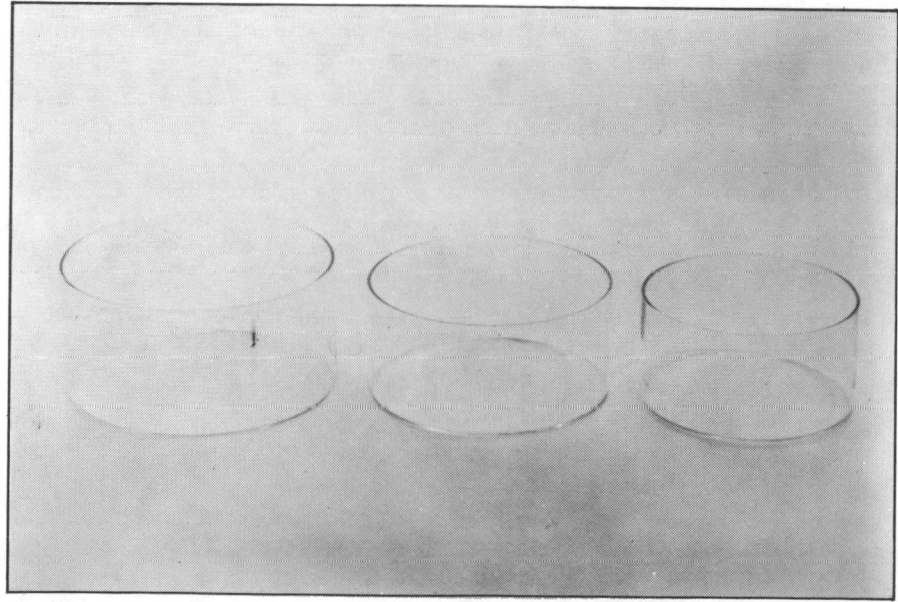

Glass Soufflé Dish Set. A soufflé may clearly be appreciated from top to bottom in a glass baking dish, as long as the temperature of the oven is set 10 degrees lower than for a porcelain or metal dish.

Savory Crêpes

BROCCOLI CRÊPES

Joanne Will

6 servings

12 CRÊPES, USING ANY STANDARD CRÊPE RECIPE, EACH 6 INCHES IN DIAMETER

Filling:
1 PACKAGE (10 OUNCES) FROZEN CHOPPED BROCCOLI
2 TABLESPOONS BUTTER
1 TABLESPOON GRATED ONION
1 TABLESPOON FLOUR

1 TEASPOON SALT
¼ TEASPOON WHITE PEPPER
⅛ TEASPOON NUTMEG
½ CUP HALF-AND-HALF
2 EGGS, SEPARATED
¼ CUP MELTED BUTTER
2 TABLESPOONS GRATED PARMESAN CHEESE

1. Make the crêpes ahead of time. Stack them with waxed paper between the crêpes. Overwrap them with plastic or foil. Refrigerate the crêpes until you are ready to assemble them.

2. Cook the broccoli following the package directions. Drain it well in a strainer and set it aside while you prepare the sauce.

3. Melt the butter in a small, heavy pan. Add the grated onion and cook it until soft. Blend in the flour and seasonings. Gradually add the half-and-half and cook, stirring constantly, until the sauce boils and thickens. Remove it from the heat.

4. Whisk the egg yolks until well blended. Add a small amount of the hot sauce to the yolks; add this mixture to the sauce. Whisk until well blended.

5. Press all moisture out of the broccoli. Blend the broccoli into the sauce.

6. Whisk the egg whites until stiff but not dry. Spoon a small amount of the egg whites into the broccoli mixture; blend them in, then carefully fold in the remaining egg white mixture.

7. Place the crêpes on a cookie sheet. Put about ¼ cup of the broccoli mixture on each crêpe. Fold or roll the filled crêpes loosely and put them, seam side down, into two buttered 2-quart shallow baking dishes.

8. Brush the crêpes with melted butter. Sprinkle them with Parmesan cheese.

9. Bake the crêpes at 375 F. for 15 to 20 minutes, or until the crêpes are puffed and browned. Serve at once.

RUSSIAN BLINIS WITH SOUR CREAM, CAVIAR OR CHOPPED HERRING

Paul Rubinstein

6 to 8 servings

Blini Batter:
2 CUPS MILK
1 TEASPOON SUGAR
1 TABLESPOON GRANULAR DRY
YEAST DISSOLVED IN ½ CUP
HOT WATER (MINIMUM 110 F.)
2 CUPS SIFTED ALL-PURPOSE
FLOUR
1 TEASPOON SALT
4 EGGS, SEPARATED
1 CUP MELTED BUTTER

Garnishes:
2 CUPS SOUR CREAM
1 CUP MELTED BUTTER
4 TO 8 OUNCES CAVIAR (RED OR
BLACK)
1 CUP CHOPPED HERRING
(OPTIONAL)

1. Heat the milk in a saucepan with the sugar almost to the boiling point, then turn off the heat and allow the mixture to cool for 10 minutes.

2. In a mixing bowl combine the dissolved yeast mixture with half of the milk, and add to it half (1 cup) of the sifted flour and ½ teaspoon salt. Mix well.

3. Cover the bowl with a damp cloth and allow the batter to rise for 30 minutes.

4. Beat the egg yolks in a small bowl, then stir them into the batter. Add the rest of the flour, milk and salt. Mix until smooth.

5. Cover the bowl again, and allow the batter to rise until it is doubled in bulk (about 1 hour).

6. Beat the egg whites until they form stiff peaks.

7. Gently fold the egg whites into the batter, together with ¼ of the melted butter. Cover and let the batter rise for 30 minutes.

8. Heat a skillet, crêpe pan or griddle. For each pancake (blini), pour a little melted butter in the pan, then 1 tablespoon batter. Flip the blini over with a spatula when bubbles burst on the top side. Cook it to a golden brown, then transfer it to a platter set in a warm oven. (If you use a pancake griddle, you can probably make about 4 to 6 blinis at a time.) Continue until all the batter has been used.

9. To serve, present the warm blinis with bowls of sour cream, melted butter, caviar and herring, if desired.

10. The classic method of eating is to spoon a little melted butter over a blini, add a spoonful of sour cream, then a little caviar or herring. Roll up, and savor!

Note: Caviar and sour cream are also excellent accompaniments to unsweetened crêpes.

CRÊPES FLORENTINE STYLE
(CRESPELLE ALLA FIORENTINA)

Giuliano Bugialli

8 servings

Crespelle, or crêpes, have appeared in Italian cookbooks since 1300, and are at least as Italian as they are French. This is the Florentine treatment most often used, though there are many others.

Crespelle:
2 TABLESPOONS BUTTER
2 CUPS SIFTED FLOUR
2 WHOLE EGGS PLUS 1 EGG YOLK
2 CUPS COLD MILK
PINCH OF SALT

To Make *Crespelle:*
1. Melt the butter in a small pan and let it stand until cool.

2. Place the flour in a crockery or plastic bowl and make a well in the flour.

3. Place the eggs and egg yolk in the well and stir very carefully, absorbing some flour from the edges of the well. Start adding the cold milk, little by little, stirring continuously with a wooden spoon until all the flour is incorporated, then add the cooled butter and salt. Mix well and place the bowl in a cool place to rest for at least 1 hour.

4. Prepare about 24 *crespelle.* For each *crespella* use ⅛ cup of batter. Using an 8½-inch crêpe pan, brush the pan with oil before cooking each one. Stack the *crespelle* as they are finished, placing a paper towel between each two. Let them stand until needed. You can prepare *crespelle* a day in advance of serving them.

Filling:
3 POUNDS FRESH SPINACH
1 POUND RICOTTA CHEESE
3 WHOLE EGGS
5 TABLESPOONS FRESHLY GRATED
  PARMESAN CHEESE
SALT TO TASTE
FRESHLY GROUND BLACK PEPPER
  TO TASTE
½ TEASPOON FRESHLY GRATED
  NUTMEG

To Make the Filling:
1. Rinse the spinach very well in cold water. Remove the large stems.

2. Heat a large pot of salted water until the water reaches the boiling point. Add the spinach and cook for about 12 minutes after the water begins to boil again.

3. Drain and cool the spinach under cold water.

4. Squeeze the spinach very dry, then chop it fine.

5. Place the spinach, along with the ricotta, eggs, and Parmesan cheese, in a

large bowl. Add salt, pepper and nutmeg and mix them all together with a wooden spoon.

White Sauce (*béchamel*):
2½ TABLESPOONS BUTTER
2½ TABLESPOONS FLOUR
2 CUPS WARM MILK
SALT TO TASTE

1. Melt the butter in a saucepan and stir in the flour. Stir, over medium heat, for 3 minutes. Slowly add the warmed milk, stirring constantly.
2. Adjust the heat so that the mixture bubbles and cook it for 4 minutes longer, stirring constantly. Add salt and let the *béchamel* cool.

For the Tomato Sauce:
1 CUP CANNED TOMATOES,
   PREFERABLY IMPORTED ITALIAN
1 TABLESPOON OLIVE OIL
SALT
PEPPER
3 OR 4 LARGE BASIL LEAVES

1. Pass the tomatoes through a food mill to remove seeds.

2. Place a small saucepan on the heat with the strained tomatoes, olive oil, salt and pepper to taste. Reduce the mixture very slowly for about 15 minutes. Add the basil leaves, each torn into 2 or 3 pieces, and let stand until cold.

To Assemble the Dish:
1. Butter two 13½-by-8¾-inch baking dishes.

2. Preheat the oven to 375 F.

3. Place 2 heaping tablespoons of the filling on one end of each *crespella,* roll it up and place it in the baking dish, arranging one next to the other.

4. Lightly drizzle the white sauce and then the tomato sauce over the *crespelle.*

5. Place the dishes in the preheated oven and bake for about 20 minutes.

6. Remove the dishes from the oven, allow the *crespelle* to cool for 2 or 3 minutes, then serve.

"STUFFED HANDKERCHIEFS"
("FAEZOLETTI RIPIENI")

Giuliano Bugialli

8 servings

In this recipe, the *crespelle* (crêpes) are not rolled up, but are placed together as little "sacks" in a baking pan. In Italian they are called "stuffed handkerchiefs" because Italian men fold their pocket handkerchiefs in this way.

Continued from preceding page

ABOUT 24 *CRESPELLE* (SEE RECIPE
PAGE 14)

Stuffing:

1 MEDIUM-SIZED CLOVE GARLIC
1 CELERY RIB
1 MEDIUM-SIZED CARROT
1 MEDIUM-SIZED RED ONION
5 TO 6 SPRIGS PARSLEY,
PREFERABLY ITALIAN
5 TABLESPOONS OLIVE OIL
3 OUNCES *PANCETTA,* OR 1½
OUNCES BOILED HAM AND 1½
OUNCES SALT PORK
½ POUND GROUND BEEF
½ POUND GROUND VEAL
SHOULDER
1 WHOLE GROUND CHICKEN
BREAST
SALT
PEPPER
1 CUP DRY RED WINE
2 WHOLE EGGS
2 TABLESPOONS FRESHLY GRATED
PARMESAN CHEESE
FRESHLY GRATED NUTMEG TO
TASTE

1. Finely chop the garlic, celery, carrot, onion and parsley.

2. Place the saucepan on medium heat with the olive oil. When the oil is warm, add the vegetables and sauté them for 5 minutes, stirring with a wooden spoon.

3. Coarsely chop the *pancetta* or ham and salt pork. Add the bits to the saucepan and sauté for 10 minutes longer. Then add the ground beef, veal and chicken to the saucepan, and with a fork try to amalgamate all the ingredients well. Add salt and freshly ground pepper and sauté for 15 minutes, stirring every so often.

4. Pour the wine over the contents of the saucepan and let it evaporate over low heat, for about 15 minutes. Remove the pan from the heat and transfer the contents to a large bowl. Let stand in a cool place, but not in the refrigerator, until needed.

White Sauce (*béchamel*):

2 TABLESPOONS BUTTER
2 TABLESPOONS FLOUR
2 CUPS MILK
SALT
4 TABLESPOONS FRESHLY GRATED
PARMESAN CHEESE

1. Prepare the *béchamel* by melting the butter in a saucepan and stirring in the flour. Stir, over medium heat, for 3 minutes. Slowly add the warmed milk, stirring constantly.

2. Adjust the heat so that the mixture bubbles and cook it for 4 minutes longer, stirring occasionally. Add salt and the Parmesan and let the *béchamel* cool.

Tomato sauce:

2 CUPS CANNED TOMATOES
1 TABLESPOON OLIVE OIL
SALT
FRESHLY GROUND BLACK PEPPER
2 TABLESPOONS FRESHLY GRATED
PARMESAN CHEESE

1. Pass the tomatoes through a food mill to remove the seeds.

2. Place a small saucepan over heat with the strained tomatoes, olive oil, and salt and pepper to taste. Reduce very slowly for about 20 minutes, then remove the pan and let the mixture stand until cool.

To assemble the dish:
1. Preheat the oven to 400 F.

2. Add 1 cup of the *béchamel* to the meat stuffing.

3. Add the eggs, Parmesan and nutmeg to the bowl containing the stuffing. Adjust the seasoning.

4. Combine the tomato sauce and the remaining *béchamel,* and place half of the tomato sauce-*béchamel* mixture in a round baking pan 12 inches in diameter.

5. Place all the *crespelle,* one by one, on the table. In the middle of each, place 1 heaping tablespoon of stuffing. Close a *crespella* by holding together its edges, making a "little sack." Stand the sacks around the sides of the baking pan, pinching each one together until a second sack is placed next to it. (Only the last placed sack must be held closed.) When the entire circumference of the baking pan is filled, the sacks will support each other and remain closed. Then make a series of inner circles in the same way, until the pan is full.

6. Pour the remaining tomato sauce-*béchamel* mixture over the little sacks and place the baking pan in the hot oven for about 20 minutes.

7. Remove the pan from the oven, allow it to cool for 5 minutes, then sprinkle the contents with Parmesan and serve.

SALMON CRÊPES WITH HOLLANDAISE SAUCE (PANNEQUET DE SAUMON)

Maurice Moore-Betty

6 servings

Crêpes:
1½ CUPS FLOUR
½ TEASPOON SALT
2½ CUPS MILK (APPROXIMATELY)
2 TABLESPOONS OIL
2 WHOLE EGGS
2 EGG YOLKS
OIL FOR COOKING

1. In a bowl, combine the flour, salt and ½ cup of the milk. Add the oil while beating, and continue beating while adding the eggs and egg yolks. Beat until the batter is smooth and thoroughly blended. Stir in the milk until the batter is the consistency of heavy cream. Allow the batter to rest for 2 hours or more.

2. Heat 1 tablespoon of the cooking oil in a 6-inch crêpe pan or skillet. Pour off excess oil, and place 2 tablespoons of batter in the center of the hot pan. Tilt

Continued from preceding page

the pan to cover the surface and cook until the batter forms tiny bubbles and begins to leave the edge of the pan. Tap the crêpe pan on the outer edge, allow the crêpe to slide half over the rim away from you, and flip the pan to turn the crêpe and brown the other side.

3. Brush the crêpe pan with enough oil to coat it lightly, and repeat the process.

Hollandaise Sauce:
3 EGG YOLKS
10 TO 12 TABLESPOONS BUTTER
SALT
PEPPER
LEMON JUICE

1. In a warm bowl, slowly mix the egg yolks thoroughly with a whisk or electric beater. Do not beat to a froth.

2. Melt the butter in a heavy saucepan. When the butter is foaming, pour it over the egg yolks in a slow stream while beating with the whisk or beater.

3. If the yolks are warm and the butter hot enough, you should now have hollandaise. If not, stand the bowl in hot water and whisk the mixture until thickened, being careful not to overheat. Season with salt, pepper and lemon juice to taste.

To Assemble and Heat:
½ POUND FRESHLY-COOKED
  SALMON
BUTTER FOR PREPARING THE
  BAKING DISH
PARSLEY FOR GARNISH

1. Heat the oven to 350 F.

2. Flake the cooked salmon coarsely and mix it with ½ cup of the hollandaise sauce.

3. Using approximately 1 tablespoon of the salmon and hollandaise mixture, fill each crêpe, turning in the sides and rolling neatly. Butter a shallow, oven-proof dish and arrange the filled crêpes in it. Heat them in the oven for 20 minutes. Spread the crêpes generously with the remaining hollandaise and glaze them under the broiler until the sauce bubbles.

4. Sprinkle the crêpes with finely chopped parsley before serving.

MANDARIN PANCAKES WITH PORK
AND LEEK FILLING

Gloria Bley Miller

4 servings

Mandarin Pancakes:
2 CUPS FLOUR PLUS EXTRA FLOUR
 FOR KNEADING
1 CUP BOILING WATER
OIL

1. Put the flour in a bowl. Make a well in the center and add the water gradually, stirring with a wooden spoon until the mixture acquires a cornmeal-like consistency.

2. Dust your hands lightly with flour and work the surface with more flour, then knead the dough until smooth and firm (about 5 minutes). Cover the dough with a damp cloth and let it stand 30 minutes.

3. Knead the dough a few times more, then roll it into a thin cylinder about 1½ inches in diameter. Cut the cylinder crosswise into 1-inch disks.

4. Flatten each disk with the palm of your hand until it is about 4 inches in diameter and ¼-inch thick. Brush lightly—on one side only—with the oil. Then form a double pancake by placing one disk atop another—oiled surfaces touching. Gently press these together with the palm of your hand.

5. Lightly flour a rolling pin and the work surface. Roll out each double pancake until very thin and about 6 inches in diameter. (Roll from the center, rotating the disk one-quarter turn after each roll for a perfectly round shape with even edges.)

6. When all the double pancakes have been rolled out, heat a small, ungreased skillet over medium heat. (The pan should be slightly larger in diameter than the pancakes, which will be cooked one at a time.) Cook each pancake for a minute on each side, until lightly browned. Immediately pull the two halves apart to separate them. (There should be 12 to 16 pancakes.)

7. Stack the individual pancakes on a platter and keep them covered with a damp cloth until they are all cooked. Cover them with foil and keep them warm in a 170 F. oven.

8. Prepare the pork and leek filling below and transfer it to a serving dish.

Pork and Leek Filling:
½ POUND LEAN PORK
3 LEEKS
2 TEASPOONS CORNSTARCH
2 TEASPOONS SOY SAUCE PLUS 1
 TABLESPOON
3 TEASPOONS MEDIUM-DRY SHERRY
3 TABLESPOONS PEANUT OIL
½ TEASPOON SALT
HOISIN SAUCE (FOUND IN
 ORIENTAL GROCERY STORES)

1. Shred the pork and put it in a bowl. Cut the leeks into 2-inch lengths.

2. In a cup, combine the cornstarch, 2 teaspoons of soy sauce and 2 teaspoons of sherry. Add to the pork and toss to blend. Let the mixture stand 15 minutes, turning occasionally.

3. Heat a wok or skillet. Add the oil and heat it. Add the pork and stir-fry it until it loses its pinkness. Add the leeks and stir-fry them to soften slightly (about 2 minutes longer).

4. In quick succession, add the salt, the remaining teaspoon of sherry and the tablespoon of soy sauce, continuing to stir-fry and blend. Remove the mixture from the pan and use as a filling for the pancakes.

5. To assemble the pancakes, take the warm pancakes from the oven and place one on a plate. Add ¼ teaspoon of *hoisin* sauce to the bottom third of the pancake and follow with about 2 tablespoons of the pork and leek filling. Fold the bottom up over the filling, then fold in each side. Roll up the pancake over the filling and eat it as a finger food.

MEAT BLINTZES

Paula J. Buchholz

4 servings

Blintz Batter:
2 EGGS
½ CUP FLOUR
½ CUP MILK
½ TEASPOON SALT
MELTED BUTTER

Filling:
1 POUND GROUND BEEF

1 ONION, CHOPPED
1 EGG
SALT
FRESHLY GROUND BLACK PEPPER
BUTTER FOR BROWNING BLINTZES

Accompaniments:
SOUR CREAM
APPLESAUCE

1. Beat the eggs well. Add the flour, milk and salt. Let the mixture stand for about 30 minutes.

2. Heat an 8-inch skillet. Lightly butter the skillet using a pastry brush. Remove the pan from the heat and pour in a few tablespoons of the batter, quickly tipping the pan back and forth until the bottom is evenly coated; pour off the excess batter. Return the skillet to the heat and cook until the bottom is browned. Turn the blintz out on a towel. Repeat with the rest of the batter. You should have about 16 blintzes.

3. To prepare the filling, cook the meat and onion until the meat is browned and the onion is translucent. Pour off any drippings.

4. Process the meat-onion mixture in a blender or food processor until the mixture is smooth. Stir in the egg, salt and pepper to taste.

5. Place several tablespoons of meat filling in the center of the cooked side of

each blintz. Fold the bottom up and the sides in over the filling, then roll up.

6. Brown the blintzes in butter over medium heat. Serve them with sour cream and applesauce.

MUSHROOM-FILLED TORTILLAS WITH CORN AND SOUR CREAM SAUCE

Diana Kennedy

4 servings

Filling:
2 TABLESPOONS BUTTER (PREFERABLY UNSALTED)
3 TABLESPOONS FINELY CHOPPED ONION
1 CLOVE GARLIC, PEELED
1 POUND MUSHROOMS
½ CUP THINLY SLICED FENNEL ROOT
SALT
PEPPER

Sauce:
3 CUPS FROZEN CORN (DO NOT DEFROST)
1½ CUPS MILK
.2 TABLESPOONS BUTTER (PREFERABLY UNSALTED)
⅔ CUP SOUR CREAM
SALT
PEPPER

To Assemble:
12 THIN, FRESHLY-MADE TORTILLAS OR CRÊPES
¾ CUP MUENSTER CHEESE
¼ CUP GRATED MUENSTER CHEESE (DOMESTIC, NOT IMPORTED)

1. Preheat the oven to 400 F. Have ready an ovenproof dish into which the 12 rolled tortillas or crêpes will just fit snugly.

2. To prepare the filling, melt the butter and wilt the onion and garlic without browning.

3. Clean and thinly slice the mushrooms. Roughly chop the sliced fennel root. Add both to the onion in the pan, season and cook for about 15 minutes over medium heat, stirring from time to time. The vegetables should be tender but still a little crisp. Season with salt and pepper to taste.

4. To prepare the sauce, blend the corn together with the milk to a very smooth purée and pass through the fine disk of a food mill.

5. Melt the butter in a saucepan over low heat and add the corn purée. Cook for about 5 minutes, stirring constantly, over low heat. Take care or it will curdle. As it begins to simmer, stir and cook for a few minutes more, until it thickens. Let the mixture cool a little before stirring in the sour cream (off the heat) and season with salt and pepper to taste. Set aside.

6. Cut the ¾ cup of cheese into thin strips and put one or two of these into each tortilla or crêpe with a large spoonful of the onion-mushroom filling. Roll the tortillas or crêpes loosely and set them side by side in the baking dish.

7. Pour the corn-sour cream sauce over them. Sprinkle with the grated cheese and set them on a rack in the top part of the oven until they are thoroughly heated through and the sauce has started to bubble.

BLINI-CRÊPES WITH SMOKED SALMON

Carole Lalli

6 appetizer servings

Crêpe Batter:
1 CUP MILK
1 CUP WATER
1⅛ CUPS UNBLEACHED WHITE
   FLOUR
⅜ CUP BUCKWHEAT FLOUR
PINCH OF SALT
2 TABLESPOONS SNIPPED DILL
4 TABLESPOONS (½ STICK)
   MELTED, COOLED BUTTER

Filling:
1 CUP HEAVY CREAM
1 TABLESPOON FRESHLY GRATED
   HORSERADISH
1 POUND BEST QUALITY SMOKED
   SALMON CUT INTO THIN SLICES
   —DANISH OR SCOTTISH IF
   POSSIBLE, BUT NOVA SCOTIA
   WILL DO

1. Whirl all the ingredients for the crêpes—except the butter—at high speed in a blender for about 30 seconds. Add the butter and whirl for 30 seconds longer. Refrigerate the batter for at least 2 hours; longer is fine.

2. When you are ready to make the crêpes, add milk or ice water, if necessary, to thin the batter. Make the crêpes, and set them aside until needed. Keep them in the refrigerator in a plastic bag if they are made in advance.

3. When ready to serve, whip the cream and add the horseradish to taste—the cream should have enough zest to cut its sweetness.

4. Place a slice of salmon on each crêpe, add a dollop of cream and roll or fold it up.

CHICKEN AND MUSHROOM CRÊPES

Nathalie Dupree

4 to 6 servings

16 TO 18 CRÊPES

Filling:
4 TABLESPOONS (½ STICK) BUTTER
2 CHOPPED ONIONS
½ POUND (2 CUPS) SLICED
   MUSHROOMS
½ PACKAGE OF FROZEN CHOPPED
   SPINACH, DEFROSTED OR
   SLIGHTLY COOKED AND WELL
   DRAINED
2 CUPS COARSELY CHOPPED
   COOKED CHICKEN OR TURKEY
6 TABLESPOONS SOUR CREAM
2 TABLESPOONS SHERRY
SALT

Sauce:
6 TABLESPOONS (¾ STICK)
   BUTTER
6 TABLESPOONS FLOUR
½ CUP SHERRY
2 CUPS CHICKEN STOCK
1 CUP MILK
¾ CUP FRESHLY GRATED
   PARMESAN CHEESE
½ CUP SWISS OR GRUYÈRE
   CHEESE
SALT

1. Melt the butter in a large frying pan. Add the onions and sauté them until they are soft. Add the mushrooms and sauté them for a few minutes. Remove the pan from the heat. Add the rest of the filling ingredients and stir. You may do this ahead of time, and refrigerate the mixture until you need it.

2. To prepare the sauce, melt the butter in another pan. Remove it from the heat, add the flour and stir until smooth. Stir in the sherry, stock and milk. Return the pan to the heat and cook, stirring constantly, until the mixture is thick and at a full boil. Reduce the heat and simmer. Add the grated cheese and salt to taste. Stir over low heat until the cheese is melted. Remove the pan from the heat, cover it with a piece of waxed paper so that a skin doesn't form. (The sauce may be frozen.)

3. When you are ready to prepare the crêpes, fill them with the warmed filling, roll them up and then place them side by side in a baking dish. Spoon some of the sauce over the crêpes and heat them in the oven (350 F.) for 15 minutes or until they are hot. Reheat the rest of the sauce gently and serve it separately.

ROQUEFORT CRÊPES

Carol Cutler

6 servings

Salvador Dali does not fit the usual image of a dairy industry lobbyist. Nevertheless, on his first trip to the United States, the flamboyant artist singlehandedly launched a boom for Roquefort cheese.

Arriving in 1940, Dali was already a celebrity, both as an artist and an eccentric. His every word was recorded. What did he think of New York? "It's a Gothic Roquefort!" With that enigmatic statement, Roquefort was on its way to fame in America. Combined here with that other French classic, the crêpe, the pungent blue-veined ewe's-milk cheese brings true Gallic *panache* to the table.

8 OUNCES ROQUEFORT OR BLUE
  CHEESE
3 TABLESPOONS HEAVY CREAM
2 TEASPOONS BRANDY
12 PREPARED CRÊPES (USE ANY
  BASIC UNSWEETENED CRÊPE
  RECIPE)
3 TABLESPOONS GRATED SWISS
  CHEESE

1. Using a fork, cream together the cheese, cream and brandy. Spread the filling over each crêpe, then roll the crêpes and place them in a buttered baking dish or pie plate. Sprinkle the crêpes with the grated Swiss cheese. (This can be done well in advance.)

2. To finish, place the dish in a 350 F. oven for about 10 minutes. Serve as soon as the crêpes begin to turn a dark golden color.

CHEESE, HAM AND ZUCCHINI LUNCHEON CRÊPES

Jane Moulton

6 servings

Basic crêpes:
1 CUP ALL-PURPOSE FLOUR
2 EGGS
½ TEASPOON SALT
1⅓ CUPS MILK
2 TABLESPOONS VEGETABLE OIL

Filling:
12 7-INCH BASIC CRÊPES
8 OUNCES (2 CUPS) GRATED
  SHARP CHEDDAR CHEESE
12 ROUND SLICES BOILED HAM
3 FRESH ZUCCHINI, ABOUT 6 OR 7
  INCHES LONG
BUTTER FOR PREPARING THE
  BAKING PAN

Sauce:
1 POUND FRESH MUSHROOMS,
  WASHED AND SLICED
2 SCALLIONS, CHOPPED FINE
8 TABLESPOONS (1 STICK) BUTTER
  OR MARGARINE
½ TEASPOON SALT
1 CUP WHIPPING CREAM

1. To make the crêpes, combine all the ingredients in a mixer bowl and beat them until smooth. Let the batter stand for 1 hour.

2. Oil a 7-inch crêpe pan and heat it until a drop of water sizzles when dropped in the pan. Use about 3 tablespoons of batter, added all at once, for each crêpe, turning and tilting the pan to cover it completely. Turn the crêpe when the bottom is nicely browned. Remove to a plate when the second side is cooked but not brown.

3. Top each crêpe with grated cheese and a slice of ham. Cut off the ends of the zucchini and quarter them lengthwise. Place a zucchini quarter on each crêpe and roll it up. Place them, crosswise, in a buttered 13-by-9-inch baking pan or put two crêpes in six individual buttered baking pans. Bake the crêpes in a preheated 350 F. oven until the cheese is melted and the zucchini is crisp-tender, about 20 to 25 minutes.

4. To make the sauce, in a large, heavy frying pan, sauté the mushrooms and onions in butter until the onions are cooked through and the mushrooms are tender, but still light in color. Sprinkle with the salt. Add the cream and simmer the sauce, uncovered, for 5 minutes.

5. Spoon the sauce over the crêpes as they are served.

Sweet Crêpes

FIG, WINE AND HONEY CRÊPE-TORTE (CRÊPE-TORTE ST.-AUBIN)

Raymond Sokolov with thanks to George Lang and Richard Olney

6 servings

1 POUND DRIED FIGS
2 CUPS RED WINE
½ TEASPOON GROUND THYME
6 TABLESPOONS HONEY
2 CUPS MILK (APPROXIMATELY)
4 EGGS, SEPARATED
1 TABLESPOON SUGAR

2 CUPS SIFTED FLOUR
BUTTER FOR FRYING THE CRÊPES
   AND COATING THE PIE DISH
2 EGG WHITES FOR MERINGUE
5 TABLESPOONS CONFECTIONERS'
   SUGAR
½ TEASPOON LEMON JUICE

1. Before preparing the crêpes, prepare the fig purée. Simply combine figs, red wine, thyme and honey in a saucepan and simmer for an hour, turning the figs occasionally. Then purée them in a blender. If the purée is too liquid to spread, boil it down further.

2. To make the crêpe batter, stir together the milk, egg yolks, sugar and flour until smooth.

3. Beat 4 egg whites until stiff, but not dry, and fold them into the batter.

4. Heat a heavy 8-inch skillet and coat it lightly with butter. Ladle about ⅓ cup of batter into the hot pan, tilting the pan to distribute it evenly. If the batter is too thick to spread easily, stir in a small extra quantity of milk.

5. Cook the crêpe until lightly browned on the bottom. You should then be able to pick up the crêpe with your fingers and turn it over gently. Brown the other side and set it on a plate. Continue in this way until all the batter is used up. You will only need to add butter to the pan for every other crêpe. All told, you should get at least 12 crêpes.

6. Butter a deep glass pie dish. Preheat the oven to 300 F.

7. Lay a crêpe on the bottom of the pie dish. Spread it with fig purée. Continue alternating crêpes and fig purée until you have used up all the crêpes and all the purée. The last crêpes should not have purée on top.

8. Beat the remaining 2 egg whites until they form soft peaks. Add the confectioners' sugar and lemon juice and continue beating until stiff. Spread the meringue mixture over the top of the crêpe-torte. Bake in the oven until the meringue begins to brown, about 15 minutes.

APPLE CRÊPES

Jane Moulton

6 servings

Basic Crêpe Recipe (see page 24)

Filling:
1 CAN (1 POUND 4-OUNCES)
  APPLES FOR PIE, DRAINED
¼ CUP LIGHT OR DARK BROWN
  SUGAR
1 TABLESPOON CORNSTARCH
½ TEASPOON CINNAMON
12 7-INCH BASIC CRÊPES

Sauce:
½ CUP HONEY
3 TABLESPOONS WATER
2 TABLESPOONS BUTTER OR
  MARGARINE
¼ CUP TOASTED SLIVERED OR
  SLICED ALMONDS

1. Cut the apples into small pieces. Combine the brown sugar, cornstarch and cinnamon; toss with the apple pieces.

2. Fill each crêpe with a scant ¼ cup of the apple mixture; roll and place them in a 13-by-9-inch baking dish. Spoon any remaining juices over the crêpes in the dish.

3. Bake, uncovered, in a preheated 350 F. oven for 15 minutes, or until the juices are bubbly.

4. Combine all the ingredients for the sauce in a small saucepan; bring to a boil and simmer for 2 minutes. Spoon the hot sauce over the crêpes and serve.

Note: Vanilla ice cream makes a good topper.

APPLE MERINGUE CRÊPES

Julie Dannenbaum

6 servings

MELTED BUTTER FOR COATING
  DISH
8 LARGE COOKING APPLES,
  PEELED, CORED AND CUT INTO
  EIGHTHS
½ CUP SUGAR, OR MORE TO
  TASTE, DEPENDING ON
  SWEETNESS OF APPLES

½ TEASPOON CINNAMON
3 TABLESPOONS CALVADOS OR
  APPLE BRANDY
16 5-INCH CRÊPES MADE FROM
  A BASIC CRÊPE RECIPE
4 EGG WHITES
¾ CUP SUGAR

1. Brush an ovenproof dish, 9 inches by 11 inches, with melted butter.

2. Place the apples, sugar, cinnamon and calvados (or brandy) in a saucepan and cook slowly until the mixture turns into a thick purée. Stir frequently.

3. Line the baking dish with slightly overlapping crêpes.

4. Spread with a mixture of the apple purée. Cover with another layer of crêpes,

and add more apple purée. End with a final layer of crêpes.

5. In a mixer, beat the egg whites until foamy, gradually adding the sugar. Beat until the mixture is very stiff and shiny.

6. Fill a pastry bag, fitted with a large star tube, with the meringue. Pipe the meringue over the top of the crêpes. It is not necessary to cover the crêpes completely.

7. Bake in a preheated 450 F. oven for 10 minutes, or until the meringue takes on a little color.

FLAMING BANANA CRÊPES

Joanne Will

6 servings

12 CRÊPES, 6 INCHES IN
  DIAMETER, MADE FROM ANY
  STANDARD CRÊPE RECIPE
½ CUP BUTTER
1 CUP PACKED BROWN SUGAR
JUICE OF 2 LEMONS (ABOUT 6
  TABLESPOONS)
JUICE OF 2 LIMES (ABOUT 3
  TABLESPOONS)
1 STICK CINNAMON
3 FIRM, RIPE BANANAS, PEELED
½ CUP GOLDEN RUM

1. Make the crêpes ahead of time. Stack them with waxed paper between the layers. Wrap the crêpes in plastic or foil. Refrigerate them until ready to heat and serve. Use plain or sweet batter, as your sweet tooth dictates. (I prefer plain crêpes.)

2. Melt the butter in a chafing dish, a *crêpes Suzette* or presentation pan, or in a skillet. Blend in the brown sugar, lemon juice, lime juice and cinnamon. Cook over moderate heat until the ingredients are blended and bubbling gently around the edge of the pan. Reduce the heat to low.

3. Put in the crêpes, one at a time. With a serving spoon and fork, fold each crêpe in half, then in quarters. Place 2 crêpes on each of six warm dessert plates.

4. Cut the bananas into halves crosswise. Cut each half into quarters. Stir them into the syrup, turning to coat each piece. Simmer just a minute, or the bananas will become too soft and overcooked.

5. Heat the rum in a small saucepan. Ignite it with a match. Pour the flaming rum into the pan with the bananas and syrup. Stir gently until the flames die down. Remove the cinnamon stick. Spoon the sauce over the crêpes and serve at once.

CRÊPES SUZETTE CORDON BLEU

Carol Cutler

Carol Cutler

4 servings

Charles Narcès, the irascible chef who ruled at the *Cordon Bleu* for so many years before his recent retirement, insisted that the only proper way to make *Crêpes Suzette* is to keep all the alcohol in the sauce rather than to ignite it to make a spectacle. *"Ça, c'est l'operette, pas la cuisine"* ("That's operetta, not cuisine").

There are probably as many strongly defended ways of making *Crêpes Suzette* as there are for mixing martinis. Even French classicists don't agree on crêpe ingredients. Some use egg yolks, others whole eggs; still others use both. There is also a difference of opinion about the liquid. Should one use milk, water, light cream or heavy cream—or a mixture of all of them? Some chefs do —and some don't—add orange liqueur to the batter. But great French chefs unanimously refuse to set crêpes afire!

Whether they are flamed or not, just announce *Crêpes Suzette* and everyone is instantly in a festive mood. There has long been a lot of mumbo-jumbo surrounding the supposedly frustrating experiences of making crêpes, but they are not difficult. They can be made early in the day and they will stay soft and mellow if the stack is covered with waxed paper or plastic wrap and kept in a cool corner of the kitchen. Freeze them? You can do it, of course, but in my opinion they won't be the same. The *Suzette* sauce, on the other hand, can be made long in advance and kept frozen.

Batter:
1¼ CUPS FLOUR
1 EGG
2 EGG YOLKS
½ TEASPOON SALT
1 TABLESPOON SUGAR
2 CUPS LUKEWARM MILK (ALL MAY
  NOT BE USED)
1 TEASPOON VANILLA
3 TABLESPOONS MELTED BUTTER
½ CUP MARGARINE FOR FRYING
  CRÊPES

1. Put the flour in a deep mixing bowl and make a well in the center of the mound of flour. In the center put the whole egg, the yolks, salt, and sugar. Mix the eggs with a wire whisk (or an electric beater) until well blended; add about ¼ cup of milk and beat this liquid mixture until quite elastic. Slowly work in the flour, adding more milk as needed to keep the batter smooth and elastic. Do not skimp on the time spent beating the batter, but beat until it becomes shiny and very elastic; about 5 minutes. Add more milk, little by little, until you have a batter that is as thin as heavy cream. Put aside for at least ½ hour.

2. Just before frying the crêpes, add the vanilla and melted butter. If the batter has thickened during the resting period, add more milk.

3. The crêpe pan must be hot before the batter is poured. To test, sprinkle a few drops of water in the pan; they should "dance." Melt the margarine in a small pot, pour some into the heated crêpe pan, swirl until the entire surface is cov-

ered with margarine, then pour the excess back into the pot.

4. Use about 3 tablespoons of batter for each crêpe; either spoon it or pour it from a small pitcher. I find the latter easier and faster. Immediately tilt the pan in all directions until a very thin film of the batter covers the entire surface. The pan should be hot enough to produce a sizzling noise when the batter hits it. This is essential to keep the crêpes paper-thin.

5. Fry each crêpe on one side for about 1 to 1½ minutes. Shake the pan to loosen the crêpe, then turn it over, with a spatula, knife, or by tossing it. Fry it for just a few seconds more and slide the finished crêpe onto a plate. This will keep the first side up, which is the prettier side and the one always presented.

6. Coat the pan with more margarine and continue frying the crêpes, stacking one on top of the other. This quantity of batter should make about 16 crêpes if they are properly thin.

Suzette Sauce:
4 TABLESPOONS (½ STICK)
 BUTTER (PREFERABLY UNSALTED)
3 TABLESPOONS SUGAR
1 FRESH ORANGE
3 TABLESPOONS ORANGE LIQUEUR
 (PREFERABLY GRAND MARNIER)

1. The sauce can be prepared by hand, in a blender, or best of all, in a food processor with the plastic blade. Cream the butter well, gradually add the sugar and continue beating. Peel the zest from the orange and reserve it. Halve and extract the juice of one-half the orange, and add the juice to the butter-sugar mixture. You will have to force the juice into the butter. (The difficulty is caused by the old principle that oil and water do not mix.) The sauce will not be completely smooth, but no matter, no one ever sees it. Add the liqueur gradually, and if the butter will hold more juice, squeeze in the other half as well.

2. Cut the zest of the orange into fine, thin strips and blanch them in 2 cups of boiling water for 3 minutes. Drain and reserve them.

Presentation of *Crêpes Suzette:*
1. Butter a serving dish that can go into the oven. Since the crêpes are stacked with the *best side up,* turn the entire stack upside down so the second side will end up being folded in.

2. Spread about a heaping teaspoon of the sauce on each crêpe. Fold it in half and then in half again; it now resembles a triangle. Place the folded crêpe on the buttered serving dish and continue with the rest, placing them so that the rounded bottom of one slightly overlaps the point of the preceding crêpe. If there is sauce left over, dot it on top of the crêpes. Scatter the blanched orange strips over the crêpes.

3. Sprinkle the crêpes with powdered sugar and just the lightest sprinkling of orange liqueur. Put the crêpes in a 350 F. oven for about 5 minutes and serve hot.

Note: With this *Suzette* method, the sauce melts right into the crêpes and is the essence of all that is subtle and delicate. The recipe works as well with tangerines.

CRÊPES SOUFFLÉES AU COGNAC

Ruth Ellen Church

4 to 5 servings

8 TO 10 LARGE, PAPER-THIN
CRÊPES, 8-INCH OR 9-INCH SIZE,
MADE FROM ANY STANDARD
CRÊPE RECIPE

Soufflé Mixture:
¼ CUP SUGAR
1 TABLESPOON FLOUR
½ CUP MILK
FEW GRAINS SALT
2 EGG YOLKS, BEATEN UNTIL PALE

4 EGG WHITES, BEATEN STIFF
1 TEASPOON VANILLA
1 TABLESPOON COGNAC

Other Ingredients:
BUTTER FOR PREPARING THE
 BAKING DISH
SUGAR FOR PREPARING THE
 BAKING DISH
½ CUP WARMED COGNAC FOR
 FLAMING

1. Have the crêpes ready.

2. Mix the sugar, flour, milk and salt in a small saucepan and cook over moderate heat, stirring constantly, until the mixture is thickened. Remove the pan from the heat and stir in the beaten egg yolks. Add the vanilla and cognac. Turn this mixture into a mixing bowl and carefully fold in the stiffly beaten egg whites.

3. Butter and sugar a glass baking dish. Fill the crêpes with the soufflé mixture and lay them side by side in the dish. Sprinkle them with sugar and slide them under the broiler for 2 or 3 minutes. Pour on warm cognac and ignite it.

MY MOTHER'S CHEESE BLINTZES

Harvey Steiman

6 servings

Blintzes:
3 EGGS, WELL BEATEN
PINCH OF SALT
1 TABLESPOON SUGAR
1½ CUPS MILK
½ CUP WATER
1 CUP UNBLEACHED WHITE FLOUR

Filling:
¼ POUND CREAM CHEESE
1 CUP POT CHEESE

1 EGG YOLK
¾ TEASPOON SALT
1 TABLESPOON MELTED BUTTER
2 TABLESPOONS SUGAR
1 TEASPOON GRATED LEMON ZEST

For Browning and Garnishing:
4 TABLESPOONS (½ STICK)
 BUTTER (APPROXIMATELY)
SOUR CREAM

1. For the blintz batter, beat the eggs well, then add salt, sugar, milk and water. Blend well. Add the flour slowly, stirring well. Let the mixture stand for 30 minutes.

2. For the filling, beat the cheese with the yolk, salt, melted butter, sugar and lemon zest.

3. Heat a 5- or 6-inch skillet over moderate heat. Melt a small pat of butter in it, just enough to coat the bottom of the pan. Pour ¼ cup of the batter into the pan, tilting it so that a thin sheet forms. Pour the excess back into the remaining batter. When the blintz is lightly browned—about 30 seconds—turn it out, browned side up, on a clean towel. As the blintzes cool, pile them up in one corner of the towel, allowing room for the remaining blintzes to cool.

   Note: If the blintz comes out too thick, add some water to the batter. If it's too fragile and falls apart, add a tablespoon of flour and beat well.

4. Repeat the cooking procedure with the remaining batter.

5. When the blintzes are cool, place a generous teaspoon (My mother's "generous teaspoon" was really about 1½ tablespoons) of filling on the browned side of a blintz. Fold two opposite sides of the blintz over the filling; then overlap the other two ends and roll up the blintz, making a neat package, rectangular in shape.

6. Repeat the procedure with the remaining blintzes.

7. Melt 1 tablespoon of butter in a frying pan over moderate heat. Arrange as many blintzes as will fit without crowding, seam side down, in the pan. Brown both sides. Repeat the procedure with the remaining blintzes.

8. Serve the blintzes with plenty of sour cream.

CRÊPES WITH FRESH PEACHES

Florence Fabricant

6 servings

Crêpe Batter:
1 CUP MILK
4 TABLESPOONS (½ STICK) BUTTER
1 TABLESPOON SUGAR
1 CUP FLOUR
2 EGGS, LIGHTLY BEATEN
1 CUP PERRIER WATER OR SPARKLING WATER

1. Heat the milk, butter and sugar together until the butter is melted and the sugar dissolved.

2. Place the flour in a bowl, make a well in the center and add the eggs. Blend them together.

3. Beat the milk mixture and Perrier until well-blended. Allow the batter to sit at least ½ hour before using.

4. Fry the crêpes, one at a time, over medium heat in a well-seasoned 6-inch crêpe pan. Use about 2 tablespoons of batter for each crêpe, tipping the pan to coat the bottom evenly. Turn each crêpe once to brown both sides. This recipe yields 18 crêpes.

Continued from preceding page

Filling:
4 CUPS PEELED, THINLY-SLICED
  FRESH PEACHES
¼ CUP GRAND MARNIER
¼ CUP ORANGE MARMALADE
CONFECTIONERS' SUGAR
½ CUP HEAVY CREAM, WHIPPED
  AND SWEETENED WITH 1
  TABLESPOON SUGAR

1. Combine the peaches with the liqueur and the marmalade. Spoon about 3 to 4 tablespoons of the peach filling into the center of each crêpe and roll the crêpe around the filling.

2. Arrange the rolled crêpes on a baking sheet or in a shallow, ovenproof baking dish and dust them liberally with confectioners' sugar.

3. Place under a hot broiler for about 5 minutes, until the tops of the crêpes are glazed and the sugar has caramelized.

4. Serve the crêpes at once with the whipped cream on the side.

RUM-RAISIN ICE CREAM CRÊPES
(CRÊPES ST. JAMES)

Nicola Zanghi

6 servings

St. James is the principal rum-producing area of Martinique.

1 CUP GRATED SWEET CHOCOLATE
½ CUP GRATED BITTER
  CHOCOLATE
¼ CUP SUGAR
¼ CUP WATER
1 TABLESPOON INSTANT COFFEE
2 TABLESPOONS BUTTER
  (PREFERABLY UNSALTED)

6 DESSERT CRÊPES, MADE FROM
  ANY STANDARD CRÊPE RECIPE
1 QUART RUM-RAISIN ICE CREAM
1 EGG YOLK
¼ CUP DARK RUM
½ CUP HEAVY CREAM

1. In a double boiler, combine the two chocolates, the sugar, water, coffee and butter and melt them.

2. Prepare the crêpes by filling them with approximately 4 to 5 tablespoons softened rum-raisin ice cream. Roll the filled crêpes and place them in the freezer until serving time.

3. Mix the egg yolk, rum and cream together. Whisk the mixture into the chocolate when it is completely melted. Return the double boiler to the heat and stir.

4. To assemble, the crêpes should be placed on heated plates and the warm sauce spooned over them.

STRAWBERRY-ALMOND CRÊPES
(CRÊPES ELIZABETH)

Ruth Ellen Church

4 servings

Crêpes:
1 CUP SIFTED FLOUR
¼ TEASPOON SALT
2 EGGS, BEATEN
1½ CUPS MILK
1 TABLESPOON MELTED BUTTER
  OR OIL

Other Ingredients:
2 TO 3 TABLESPOONS BUTTER FOR
  WARMING CRÊPES
¼ CUP TOASTED SLIVERED
  ALMONDS
WHIPPED CREAM FLAVORED WITH
  ALMOND EXTRACT OR LIQUEUR

Filling:
1 PINT OF STRAWBERRIES, SLICED
SUGAR TO SWEETEN

1. Whirl the first set of ingredients in a blender for a few seconds, or beat smooth. Let the batter stand for 1 hour.

2. Use your crêpe pan according to the maker's directions, or pour the batter onto a hot greased griddle, or into a 6- or 7-inch omelet pan lightly brushed with butter, using only enough batter (about 1½ tablespoons) to coat the surface. Cook on both sides until golden brown. Make the crêpes ahead and reheat them with the filling.

3. Fill the crêpes with the lightly sweetened strawberries, lay them side by side in a chafing dish in which you have melted 2 or 3 tablespoons butter, sprinkle with the almonds and warm thoroughly. Serve with the flavored whipped cream.

WHOLE WHEAT CRÊPES WITH
BROWN SUGAR SAUCE

Elizabeth Colchie

3 servings

Crêpe batter:
¾ CUP MILK
¼ CUP WHOLE WHEAT FLOUR
1 EGG
1½ TABLESPOONS MELTED BUTTER
¼ CUP PEELED, CHOPPED APPLE
BIG PINCH SALT

1. Combine the ingredients in the order listed in the container of a blender and purée them until no apple pieces remain. Cover the batter and refrigerate it for several hours or longer.

2. Heat a 5- to 6-inch crêpe pan and brush it very lightly with melted butter. Pour

Continued from preceding page

slightly less than ⅓ cup of the batter into a measure and, using half this amount (that is, about 2½ tablespoons), pour the batter into the buttered pan. Immediately tilt to cover the surface of the pan and let the crêpe "bake" for 30 seconds over moderate heat, or until the top of the crêpe is dry and the bottom is browned.

3. Turn the crêpe and cook it for 15 to 20 seconds. Flip the crêpe onto a plate; place it in a warm oven and repeat the process until all of the batter is used and you have a stack of about 9 crêpes in the oven. Make the sauce.

Sauce:
¼ CUP LIGHT BROWN SUGAR
2 TABLESPOONS BUTTER
1 TABLESPOON DARK RUM
1 TEASPOON LEMON JUICE

1. Combine all the ingredients in a small, heavy skillet. Bring them to a boil, stirring. Simmer for 2 minutes.

2. Fold the crêpes into quarters and place them on 3 heated dessert plates. Pour the sauce evenly over the crêpes and serve immediately.

ORANGE-FLOWER BREAKFAST CRÊPES

Elizabeth Colchie

2 generous servings

½ CUP MILK
6 TABLESPOONS HEAVY CREAM
2 LARGE EGGS
4 TABLESPOONS SUGAR
2 TABLESPOONS ORANGE-FLOWER WATER (USE A GOOD, POTENT BRAND)

½ CUP INSTANT-TYPE FLOUR
⅛ TEASPOON SALT
PLAIN OR ORANGE-FLAVORED CONFECTIONERS' SUGAR (SEE NOTE)

1. Add the ingredients to the blender container in the order listed, except for the confectioners' sugar. Blend at high speed for 15 to 20 seconds, scraping down the sides of the container if necessary.

2. Heat a 5- to 6-inch crêpe pan over moderate heat and brush very lightly with butter. Pour in approximately 3 tablespoons of batter at a time and quickly tilt the pan to cover it completely. Cook the crêpe for about 30 seconds, or until the top is dry; turn it and bake for about 15 seconds, or until just golden.

3. Continue, using two pans if you have them. Sift confectioners' sugar over each crêpe.

Note: To prepare orange-flavored confectioner's sugar, bury a wide, 3-inch-long strip of dried orange rind in a cup of sugar in a jar with a lid. In about 3 days the rind will impart its fragrance to the sugar; the flavor will last indefinitely.

MANDARIN ORANGE CRÊPES

Emanuel and Madeline Greenberg

4 to 6 servings

Crêpes:
2 EGGS, PLUS 1 EGG YOLK
¾ CUP MILK
2 TABLESPOONS COGNAC OR DARK
   RUM
2 TABLESPOONS MELTED BUTTER
¾ CUP FLOUR
2 TEASPOONS SUGAR
¼ TEASPOON SALT
1 TABLESPOON MELTED BUTTER
   FOR COATING THE PAN

1. Beat the eggs and the yolk together until they are foamy. Add the other ingredients; beat until smooth. Let the batter stand about 1 hour.

2. Heat a crêpe pan and coat it lightly with butter. Pour 2 tablespoons of batter into the pan, tilting and turning to spread it.

3. When the crêpe is set and the underside is lightly browned, turn it and brown the second side lightly. Repeat the process with the rest of the batter. You should have 12 crêpes.

Sauce and Assembly:
12 CRÊPES
¾ CUP APRICOT PRESERVES
2 CANS (11 OUNCES EACH)
   MANDARIN ORANGES
4 TABLESPOONS (½ STICK)
   BUTTER
¼ CUP MANDARINE NAPOLEON OR
   OTHER TANGERINE LIQUEUR
¼ CUP COGNAC OR DARK RUM

1. Spread each crêpe with the preserves and fold it in quarters. Drain the oranges, saving the syrup.

2. Heat the butter in a chafing dish, pan or skillet. Add the drained oranges and brown lightly. Add Mandarine Napoleon and ¼ cup syrup from the oranges. Cook, stirring occasionally, until the liquid comes to a boil.

3. Push the oranges to the side of the pan, add the folded crêpes and baste them with the sauce until they are heated through. Spoon the oranges around and over the crêpes.

4. Warm the cognac or rum, ignite it, then pour it, flaming, into the pan. Serve the crêpes at once.

Savory Hot Soufflés

CORN SOUFFLÉ

Diana Kennedy

4 servings

This type of soufflé does not rise as spectacularly as the lighter and more traditional cheese soufflé, but it is moister. It is baked in a water bath and, for this, I suggest putting a roasting pan on a rack in the lower half of the oven. There should be about 1 inch of hot water in the roasting pan; the water should rise half way up the side of the dish.

Corn Mixture:
- 1½ TABLESPOONS BUTTER (PREFERABLY UNSALTED), PLUS BUTTER FOR PREPARING THE SOUFFLÉ DISH
- 1 SMALL CLOVE GARLIC, PEELED AND FINELY CHOPPED
- 2 TABLESPOONS FINELY CHOPPED ONION
- 1½ CUPS FROZEN CORN KERNELS (DO NOT DEFROST) OR VERY FRESH YOUNG CORN
- 2 FRESH GREEN CHILIES, FINELY CHOPPED (OPTIONAL)
- SALT TO TASTE
- FRESHLY GROUND BLACK PEPPER TO TASTE

White Sauce Base:
- 2 TABLESPOONS BUTTER
- 1 HEAPING TABLESPOON FLOUR
- ½ CUP WARM MILK
- 4 LARGE (2-OUNCE) EGGS, SEPARATED

1. Place the waterbath in the oven. Preheat the oven to 375 F. Butter a 1½-quart soufflé dish lavishly.

2. Prepare the corn mixture by melting the butter and wilting the garlic and onion without browning. Add the corn kernels and the chilies; season and cook until tender, but still crisp, about 5 minutes.

3. Prepare the white sauce base by melting the butter and adding the flour, letting it froth up well and stirring constantly for a few minutes.

4. Gradually stir in the warmed milk and cook the mixture until it thickens, stirring constantly. Add the corn mixture and adjust seasonings, if necessary.

5. Separate the eggs and stir the yolks, one at a time, thoroughly into the corn base.

6. Beat the egg whites until they are stiff, but not dry. Add 1 large spoonful of the whites to the corn base and stir in well. Fold in the remaining beaten whites and pour the mixture into the prepared dish.

7. Place the dish in the waterbath and bake for about 40 minutes, or until the

soufflé Is just firm, and is nicely browned on top. (For those who like it creamier inside, reduce the cooking time accordingly.)

8. Serve the soufflé immediately, either by itself or with a light tomato sauce, or with a little salted sour cream.

HAM SOUFFLÉ

Harvey Steiman

6 appetizer servings/2 to 3 main course servings

White Sauce (*béchamel*):
1½ TABLESPOONS BUTTER
1½ TABLESPOONS FLOUR
½ CUP WARM MILK
SALT
PEPPER
PINCH OF NUTMEG
ONION SLICE (OPTIONAL)
WHOLE CLOVE (OPTIONAL)

1. Melt the butter in a small saucepan over moderate heat. Stir in the flour and cook, stirring, until the raw-flour aroma dissipates, about 3 to 4 minutes.

2. Add the warm milk and stir until thick. Simmer for 10 minutes, then season the *béchamel* with salt and pepper to taste and add a pinch of nutmeg.

   Note: For more flavor, you may heat a slice of onion and a whole clove in the milk. Strain the milk before adding it to the butter-flour mixture.

1 TEASPOON BUTTER
1 TO 2 TABLESPOONS GRATED
  PARMESAN CHEESE
7½ OUNCES CANNED HAM SPREAD
  (OR LEAN HAM GROUND OR
  CHOPPED VERY FINE)
½ CUP THICK *BÉCHAMEL*
DASH OF TABASCO OR HOT SAUCE
1 TO 2 GRINDINGS BLACK PEPPER
3 EGGS, SEPARATED

1. Preheat the oven to 375 F. Butter and coat a 1½-quart soufflé mold or straight-sided baking dish with the grated cheese.

2. Mix the ham with 2 tablespoons of the *béchamel* or purée it in a food processor. Season with Tabasco and pepper. Add the remaining *béchamel* and beat in the egg yolk.

3. Beat the egg whites until stiff, then fold them into the ham mixture. Transfer the mixture to the baking dish.

4. Bake 20 to 25 minutes. Serve the soufflé immediately.

INDIVIDUAL CHEESE SOUFFLÉS WITH CREAM OR MUSHROOM SAUCE

Paul Rubinstein

6 servings

Sauce:
1 1-OUNCE PACKAGE EUROPEAN
  DRIED MUSHROOMS
2 CUPS BOILING WATER
6 TABLESPOONS (¾ STICK)
  BUTTER
½ POUND FRESH WHITE
  MUSHROOMS, SLICED VERY THIN
1 TABLESPOON LEMON JUICE
¼ TEASPOON FRESHLY GROUND
  BLACK PEPPER
2 TABLESPOONS FLOUR
½ CUP HEAVY CREAM

Soufflé:
4 TABLESPOONS (½ STICK)
  BUTTER
4 TABLESPOONS GRATED
  PARMESAN CHEESE
1 CUP MILK
3 TABLESPOONS FLOUR
½ TEASPOON SALT
5 EGGS, SEPARATED
1 CUP GRATED SWISS CHEESE

1. The sauce should be completely prepared first and kept warm in a sauceboat, ready to serve as soon as the soufflés come to the table.

2. Put the dried mushrooms into the boiling water and let them soak until they are quite soft and the water turns the color of strong tea.

3. Melt 4 tablespoons of the butter in a skillet, add the sliced fresh mushrooms, lemon juice and pepper, toss and simmer over medium heat until the mushroom slices are soft and have yielded their liquid. Set the skillet aside, off the heat.

4. Remove the soaked mushrooms from the liquid (reserve the liquid), chop them fine and add them to the skillet.

5. In a saucepan, melt the remaining 2 tablespoons of butter, add the flour, stir it into a paste over medium heat and cook for 2 minutes, stirring constantly to avoid browning.

6. Add the mushroom liquid a little at a time, stirring until it is absorbed. The result should be a slightly thickened sauce.

7. Add the contents of the skillet (mushrooms and liquid) to the saucepan, then stir in the heavy cream. Bring to a simmer (do not allow to boil), then transfer the sauce to the warm sauceboat and keep warm.

8. Using 1 tablespoon of butter, lightly coat the insides of 6 individual soufflé dishes or ramekins, each about 3½ inches in diameter and 2 inches deep. Sprinkle them with some of the grated Parmesan cheese, making sure a fine coating of it adheres to the sides of the ramekins.

9. Preheat the oven to 400 F.

10. Boil the cup of milk in a saucepan, remove from the heat and have ready.

11. Melt the remaining 3 tablespoons of butter in a saucepan, add the flour, cook for 2 minutes, stirring well; do not allow it to brown.

12. Off the heat, add the hot milk to the butter-flour mixture and beat until well blended. Stir in the salt, return to the heat and stir until the batter thickens.

13. Off the heat, beat the egg yolks into the batter, adding them one at a time.

14. Beat the egg whites until they form stiff peaks. Stir a spoonful of the egg whites into the batter, then fold in the rest of the whites gently.

15. Stir the grated Swiss cheese into the batter.

16. Pour the batter into the ramekins, filling them about ¾ full. Sprinkle the tops with the remaining Parmesan cheese.

17. Bake the soufflés in the middle of the preheated oven for about 30 minutes, or until nicely puffed up and browned. Serve the soufflés in the ramekins with the sauce on the side.

Note: For soufflés, it is very nice to have an oven with a glass door; if you do not have one, wait the full 30 minutes before looking!

GRITS SOUFFLÉ WITH PARMESAN CHEESE AND BACON

Elizabeth Colchie

3 to 4 luncheon servings/4 to 5 side dish servings

1 CUP WATER
1 CUP MILK
½ TEASPOON SALT
½ CUP HOMINY GRITS
3 STRIPS BACON, CHOPPED
1 TABLESPOON BUTTER
¼ TEASPOON TABASCO SAUCE OR
    HOT SAUCE
3 EGG YOLKS
½ TEASPOON BAKING POWDER
½ CUP GRATED PARMESAN
    CHEESE
3 EGG WHITES

1. In a heavy saucepan combine the water, milk and salt; bring to a boil. Add the grits gradually, keeping the liquid at a full boil and stirring constantly. Lower the heat as far as possible, cover the pot and cook for 15 minutes, stirring occasionally.

2. Meanwhile, brown the bacon in a small skillet. When the grits have finished cooking, stir in the bacon and bacon fat, butter and Tabasco.

3. In a small bowl beat the yolks and baking powder until pale and thick; stir the mixture into the grits vigorously; add the Parmesan.

4. Beat the whites until stiff peaks form; stir a big spoonful into the grits mixture; fold in the remainder. Turn the mixture into a buttered 1½-quart soufflé dish or charlotte mold. Bake in a preheated 350 F. oven for 40 minutes, or until delicately browned on top.

LOBSTER SOUFFLÉ

Nan Mabon

4 servings

1½ CUPS FISH STOCK OR 1 CUP
  CLAM JUICE AND ½ CUP WATER
½ CUP WHITE WINE
1 STALK CELERY, ROUGHLY
  CHOPPED
1 SMALL ONION, ROUGHLY
  CHOPPED
1 MEDIUM-SIZED CARROT,
  ROUGHLY CHOPPED
3 PARSLEY STEMS
6 PEPPERCORNS
1 IMPORTED BAY LEAF
⅛ TEASPOON THYME
1 1½ POUND LIVE LOBSTER
4 TABLESPOONS (½ STICK)
  BUTTER

3 TABLESPOONS FLOUR
1 TABLESPOON TOMATO PASTE
½ CUP MILK
4 EGG YOLKS
½ CUP SWISS CHEESE, GRATED
  (PREFERABLY IMPORTED)
5 EGG WHITES

Lobster *Velouté* Sauce:
2 TABLESPOONS BUTTER
1 TABLESPOON FLOUR
REMAINING FISH-COOKING LIQUID
¼ CUP HEAVY CREAM
1 TABLESPOON LEMON JUICE
SALT
WHITE PEPPER

1. Put the stock, white wine, celery, onion and carrot in the bottom of a steamer or a casserole with a cover; one that is large enough to accommodate the lobster. Add parsley stems, peppercorns, bay leaf and thyme. Lower the steamer basket (or substitute a wire rack) and bring the contents to a simmer on top of the stove. Place the lobster inside, cover, and simmer for 10 minutes. Remove the cover and allow to cool.

2. Strain the cooled liquid into a large measuring cup, pressing down to extract all the juices. Then discard the vegetables.

3. Crack the cooled lobster on a platter, carefully saving the juices. Put the tomalley (green liver), and coral, if any, in a small bowl. Remove the meat from the claws, tail and legs, and chop it fine. Scrape the white, curd-like substance that clings to the empty shells into the liquid. Pour all accumulated juices into the measuring cup.

4. Melt 3 tablespoons of butter in an enameled or stainless-steel saucepan, stir in the flour and cook, stirring, for a minute without browning. Add the tomato paste, then whisk in the milk and ½ cup of the cooking liquid. Bring to a boil. When very thick, take off the heat and stir in the egg yolks, lobster meat, tomalley and coral. Preheat the oven to 400 F.

5. Coat an oval 10-by-1½-inch gratin pan with the remaining tablespoon of butter and sprinkle it with half of the cheese.

6. Whip the whites until they form stiff peaks. Stir a tablespoon of whites into the lobster base, then quickly and carefully fold in the rest. Pour the mixture into the prepared pan and sprinkle the top with the rest of the cheese. Place the pan on a metal cookie sheet and bake for 20 minutes.

7. To prepare the sauce, melt 1 tablespoon of the butter in a heavy saucepan.

8. Stir in the flour and cook over gentle heat for a minute.

9. Stir in the remaining fish-cooking liquid, add the cream and allow to simmer over low heat for about 10 minutes.

10. Just before serving, stir in the lemon juice and remaining tablespoon of butter. Add salt and pepper to taste. Serve the sauce separately.

ZUCCHINI AND HERB SOUFFLÉ (KOLOKITHAKIA SOUFFLÉ)

Vilma Liacouras Chantiles

6 servings

Delicious with zucchini and herbs, or you may substitute cooked asparagus tips or spinach for an equally delectable soufflé.

½ STALK CELERY, MINCED
PINCH OF THYME
SALT
3 TO 4 SMALL ZUCCHINI, SCRUBBED, STEMS CUT OFF
2 SPRIGS CHOPPED PARSLEY
1 SPRIG CHOPPED FRESH BASIL OR DILL
4 TABLESPOONS (½ STICK) SWEET BUTTER OR MARGARINE (PREFERABLY UNSALTED)
4 TABLESPOONS ALL-PURPOSE FLOUR

1¼ CUPS WARM MILK
GRATED NUTMEG OR ALLSPICE
FRESHLY GROUND PEPPER
⅓ CUP CRUMBLED *FETA* CHEESE
4 EGGS, SEPARATED, AT ROOM TEMPERATURE
3 ADDITIONAL EGG WHITES, AT ROOM TEMPERATURE
¼ TEASPOON CREAM OF TARTAR
FRESH DILL FOR GARNISH

1. Combine the celery, thyme and ½ teaspoon salt in 1½ cups of water in a saucepan and bring to a boil. Add the zucchini. Parboil for 5 minutes, then drain. Cut the zucchini into rings, or chop it. There should be a heaping cupful.

2. Mix in the parsley, and the basil or dill. Heat the butter or margarine in a heavy pan for 1 minute without browning. Add the flour and stir over medium heat until the mixture bubbles. Remove from the heat.

3. Add the milk and whisk steadily until the mixture is smooth. Return it to moderate heat and cook until the sauce boils. Season it with a little salt, the spice and pepper and add the *feta*. Cool slightly.

4. Beating steadily, add the egg yolks, one at a time. Mix the zucchini and herbs into the sauce and stir.

5. Beat the 7 egg whites with the cream of tartar until they are shiny and form peaks. Stir about one-quarter of the whites into the zucchini-sauce mixture. Then, fold in the remaining whites, using an over-and-under motion to avoid losing air.

6. Spoon the mixture into a buttered 1½-quart soufflé dish or use individual soufflé dishes. Bake on a baking sheet in the center of a moderately hot oven (400 F.) for 25 to 30 minutes. (Small soufflés will bake in 10 to 13 minutes.) Garnish with the dill and serve immediately.

BROCCOLI SOUFFLÉ

Florence Fabricant

4 servings

6 TABLESPOONS (¾ STICK) BUTTER
2 TABLESPOONS BREAD CRUMBS
½ CUP CHOPPED ONION
1¼ CUPS COOKED BROCCOLI
3 TABLESPOONS FLOUR
1 CUP MILK
4 EGG YOLKS, AT ROOM TEMPERATURE

½ CUP GRATED PARMESAN CHEESE
1 TEASPOON SALT, OR TO TASTE
PINCH OF NUTMEG
FRESHLY GROUND BLACK PEPPER
3 EGG WHITES, AT ROOM TEMPERATURE

1. Butter a 1½-quart soufflé dish with 1 tablespoon of the butter and sprinkle it with bread crumbs.

2. Melt 2 tablespoons of the butter in a skillet, add the onion and sauté it until it is soft, but not brown.

3. Combine the onion and broccoli and force them through a food mill or sieve or purée them in a food processor. You should have about 1 cup of purée.

4. Preheat the oven to 400 F.

5. Melt the remaining butter in a heavy saucepan, add the flour and stir for several minutes over medium heat to blend. Scald the milk in a small pan and slowly pour it into the saucepan, stirring with a whisk. Continue cooking, stirring with a whisk, until the sauce is thick and smooth.

6. Beat the egg yolks into the sauce one at a time. Stir in all but 2 tablespoons of the cheese, add the broccoli purée and season with salt, nutmeg and pepper. (Over-season the mixture slightly because the egg whites will dilute it.)

7. Beat the egg whites until stiff, but not dry, and fold them into the broccoli mixture. Pour into the prepared dish and dust with the remaining 2 tablespoons of cheese.

8. Place in the oven, lower the heat to 375 F. and bake for 30 minutes. Serve at once.

BLENDER SMOKED HADDOCK SOUFFLÉ

Carol Cutler

6 servings

I have developed a new technique for producing a foolproof, hot, puffy soufflé. The entire procedure is done in the blender. There is no sauce base, no beating of egg whites, and no need to prepare the soufflé at the last minute. It can stand in the dish for hours waiting to be popped into the oven. The secret of all this magic is to use cream cheese in the batter. It provides the necessary body and thickening quality and can be processed in the blender.

½ POUND SMOKED HADDOCK	2 EGG WHITES
1 SMALL ONION	DASH OF TABASCO OR HOT SAUCE
PEPPER	½ TEASPOON WORCESTERSHIRE
1 CUP MILK (APPROXIMATELY)	SAUCE
½ CUP WATER	½ CUP HEAVY CREAM
(APPROXIMATELY)	12 OUNCES CREAM CHEESE
6 EGGS	1 TABLESPOON BUTTER

1. Rinse the haddock under cold running water, then place it in a small, heavy non-aluminum pot that will hold it snugly. Slice the onion in thick slices and scatter the slices over and under the fish. Sprinkle with pepper. Pour in enough milk and water to cover the fish. Cover the pot with a lid and place it over medium heat. Bring the liquid slowly to the boil and simmer the fish gently for 5 minutes. Let the fish cool slightly in the milk.

2. In the blender, put the eggs, egg whites, Tabasco or hot sauce, Worcestershire sauce, cream, pepper, and about 2 tablespoons of the cooked onions. Blend thoroughly.

3. Lift the fish out of the milk and flake it, removing any bones that may remain. With the blender running, add the fish. Again, with the blender running, add the cream cheese. When all the ingredients have been thoroughly blended, give a final whirl at high speed.

4. Butter a 1½-quart soufflé dish. Pour the batter in the dish. (The batter must not completely fill the dish; there should be about ¼ inch of space left above the batter level.) The soufflé can stand for 2 to 3 hours before being baked. If kept longer than that, it should be refrigerated, but allow an extra 5 to 10 minutes of baking time.

5. Preheat the oven to 375 F. Bake the soufflé for 40 to 50 minutes, depending on how firm you prefer it. Test for firmness by shaking the dish; moist batter will jiggle. When it is ready, serve it at once.

OYSTER SOUFFLÉ

Helen McCully

6 servings

5 TABLESPOONS BUTTER	1 CUP CRACKER CRUMBS (ABOUT
¾ CUP FRESHLY GRATED	12 SALTED CRACKERS)
PARMESAN CHEESE (3 OUNCES)	FRESHLY GROUND WHITE PEPPER
18 OYSTERS IN THEIR LIQUOR	4 TABLESPOONS FLOUR
MILK	SALT
⅓ CUP OLIVE OIL	6 EGGS, SEPARATED
1 SMALL CLOVE GARLIC, PEELED,	3 EXTRA EGG WHITES
CRUSHED AND MINCED	

1. Prepare a 1½-quart soufflé dish by coating it with 1 tablespoon of butter and then sprinkling it with 2 tablespoons of Parmesan cheese and refrigerate it.

2. Strain the liquor from the oysters through a double layer of cheesecloth into

Continued from preceding page

a measuring cup. Purée 6 of the oysters in an electric food processor or blender, then combine them with the oyster liquor. You should have 1 cup. If not, add sufficient milk to make a full cup. Set it aside to use for making the white sauce.

3. Place ½ cup of the grated cheese in a bowl. Put the olive oil and garlic in a second bowl. Season the cracker crumbs well with pepper and place them in a third bowl.

4. Pat the remaining 12 oysters dry with paper towels. Dip each oyster first into the cheese, then into the oil and finally, roll it in cracker crumbs. Set them aside on a tray.

5. Melt the remaining 4 tablespoons of butter in a heavy saucepan. Stir in the flour; stir constantly until the flour is cooked, but not browned. Add the reserved cup of oyster liquor and salt and pepper to taste. Stir until the mixture is thick, smooth and bubbling. Remove it from the heat and allow it to cool a bit.

6. With a wire whisk, beat the 6 yolks, one at a time, into the lukewarm sauce. (The soufflé can be prepared to this point and set aside, sealed with plastic wrap.)

7. Beat the 9 egg whites with an electric beater (or in an electric mixer) until they form firm, shiny peaks. With a wire whisk, vigorously whip about a third of the whites into the sauce. Then fold in the remaining whites with a rubber scraper.

8. Pour half the soufflé mixture into the prepared dish. Arrange the oysters on top, cover with the remaining mixture and sprinkle the top with the remaining cheese.

9. Bake the soufflé in a preheated 350 F. oven for 30 to 35 minutes.

SPINACH SOUFFLÉ

Raymond Sokolov

4 servings

BUTTER FOR PREPARING THE
  SOUFFLÉ DISH
1 10-OUNCE BAG OF SPINACH
2 TABLESPOONS BUTTER
2 TABLESPOONS FLOUR
2 TABLESPOONS GRATED
  PARMESAN CHEESE

½ CUP MILK
4 EGGS, SEPARATED
SALT
FRESHLY GROUND BLACK PEPPER
NUTMEG

1. Preheat the oven to 425 F. Butter a 1½-quart soufflé dish.

2. Trim off the large stalks and wash the spinach. Shake off as much water as possible. Blanch the spinach in simmering water in an uncovered saucepan. Stir it frequently and do not overcook it. Drain it, then chop it fine. Measure out ¾ cup and squeeze out any remaining moisture.

3. Melt the butter in a saucepan. Add the flour and 1 tablespoon of the cheese. Heat through, then add the milk and stir until smooth and thickened. Stir in the chopped spinach, off the heat.

4. Stir the egg yolks into the hot, but not boiling, sauce; season with salt, pepper and nutmeg. Transfer the mixture to a large bowl.

5. Beat the egg whites until they are stiff, but not dry. Stir a small amount into the spinach mixture to lighten it. Fold in the rest of the whites.

6. Pour the soufflé mixture into the prepared dish. Sprinkle the top with the remaining cheese. Bake for 15 minutes, or until the top of the soufflé has crusted over nicely. The center will be slightly runny. Serve immediately.

SAVORY CHEESE SOUFFLE, GREEK STYLE
(TYRI SOUFFLE)

Vilma Liacouras Chantiles

4 to 5 servings

3 TABLESPOONS BUTTER OR MARGARINE (PREFERABLY UNSALTED)
3 TABLESPOONS ALL-PURPOSE FLOUR
1 CUP WARM MILK
NUTMEG OR 1 TABLESPOON CHOPPED FRESH MINT OR DILL
WHITE PEPPER (OPTIONAL)

4 EGGS, SEPARATED, AT ROOM TEMPERATURE
1 CUP CRUMBLED *FETA* CHEESE, OR A COMBINATION OF GRATED *MIZITHRA* AND *KEFALOTYRI* CHEESES (SEE NOTE BELOW)
2 ADDITIONAL EGG WHITES, AT ROOM TEMPERATURE
¼ TEASPOON CREAM OF TARTAR

1. Over low heat, melt the butter or margarine in a heavy pan and stir in the flour. Cook over very low heat, stirring constantly, without browning, until the mixture bubbles. Remove the pan from the heat and add the milk, stirring with a whisk until smooth.

2. Return the pan to medium heat, stirring, and bring the contents to a boil. Grate about ¼ nutmeg (¼ teaspoon) into the sauce and season with white pepper. (If you prefer, use the chopped mint or dill.) Remove the pan from the heat, cool the mixture slightly, then add the yolks one at a time, beating steadily. Stir in the cheese and allow the soufflé base to rest while you prepare the whites.

3. Using an electric or rotary hand beater, beat the 6 egg whites with the cream of tartar until they are shiny and form peaks. Stir 2 large tablespoons into the cheese mixture. Fold the remaining whites carefully into the mixture, using a rubber scraper. Avoid losing air from the whites.

4. Pour the mixture into a buttered 1½-quart soufflé dish. Bake on a baking sheet in the center of a 400 F. oven for 25 minutes. Serve immediately.

Note: You may substitute hard ricotta and *romano locatelli* for *mizithra* and *kefalotyri.*

Sweet Hot Soufflés

AUSTRIAN-STYLE DESSERT PUFFS

Elizabeth Colchie

4 servings

2 TABLESPOONS LEMON JUICE
3 TABLESPOONS WATER
1 TEASPOON CORNSTARCH
½ TEASPOON GRATED LEMON PEEL
3 TABLESPOONS BUTTER (PREFERABLY UNSALTED)
3 TABLESPOONS SUGAR
4 EGG WHITES
⅛ TEASPOON CREAM OF TARTAR
⅛ TEASPOON SALT
3 TABLESPOONS SUPERFINE SUGAR
2 EGG YOLKS
1 TABLESPOON FLOUR
1 TEASPOON VANILLA EXTRACT
VANILLA-FLAVORED POWDERED SUGAR (SEE NOTE BELOW)

1. In a cup, mix together the lemon juice, water, cornstarch and lemon peel; stir to dissolve the cornstarch.

2. In a small skillet, melt the butter; stir in the sugar; stir in the cornstarch mixture and stir over medium heat until the mixture boils. Pour the sauce into a buttered oval baking-serving dish, about 10 inches long and 7 inches across the center and about 1½ inches high; place the dish in the oven and turn the heat to 350 F.

3. As soon as the dish is in the oven, beat the egg whites until they are frothy; add the cream of tartar and salt and beat to form stiff peaks; gradually beat in the superfine sugar.

4. In a small bowl, beat the yolks until they are light and thick; beat in the flour and vanilla. Stir about one-quarter of the whites thoroughly into the yolks. Fold the yolk mixture into the whites.

5. Spoon 4 roughly egg-shaped mounds across the hot sauce to reach crosswise from one side of the dish to the other. Bake for about 12 minutes in the preheated oven, or until the puffs are browned, but soft inside.

6. Sprinkle with the powdered sugar and serve immediately, spooning some of the lemon sauce on each serving.

Note: To make vanilla-flavored powdered sugar, place a vanilla bean in powdered sugar in a jar with a tight-fitting lid. In a few days the sugar will become fragrant with vanilla, and it will keep indefinitely.

NORTHERN ITALIAN ALMOND MACAROON SOUFFLÉ

Paula Wolfert

4 servings

Here is a good soufflé using the famous Italian *amaretti di Saronno*, vanilla-flavored almond macaroons. It is flavored, too, with *Amaretto*, liqueur distilled from bitter almonds. This soufflé is very nice with a hot chocolate sauce.

3 TABLESPOONS ALL-PURPOSE
   FLOUR
¾ CUP MILK
½ CUP SUGAR
4 EGG YOLKS
⅓ CUP CRUMBLED ITALIAN
   ALMOND MACAROONS
½ TEASPOON VANILLA EXTRACT
2 TABLESPOONS *AMARETTO*
6 EGG WHITES
PINCH OF SALT
CONFECTIONERS' SUGAR

1. In a heavy saucepan, beat the flour with 3 tablespoons milk until smooth. Beat in the remaining milk and the sugar. Cook, stirring, until the mixture boils. Beat vigorously over medium heat until it is thick and smooth. Allow the mixture to cool.

2. Beat in the egg yolks, one by one. Then add the crumbled macaroons, the vanilla and the *Amaretto*.

3. Preheat the oven to 400 F.

4. Beat the egg whites with a pinch of salt until stiff. Stir ¼ of the beaten egg whites into the base to lighten it. Then fold in the remaining whites. Transfer to a 1½-quart buttered and sugared soufflé mold and bake for 30 to 35 minutes. After the first 10 minutes, lower the oven heat to 350 F. Remove the soufflé when it is puffy and golden brown, about 20 minutes.

5. Dust with confectioners' sugar and serve at once. Pass the chocolate sauce separately.

Chocolate Sauce (1 cup):
4 OUNCES SWEET COOKING
   CHOCOLATE
½ CUP WATER
2 TABLESPOONS BUTTER
   (PREFERABLY UNSALTED)
1 TEASPOON VANILLA EXTRACT
2 TO 3 TABLESPOONS HEAVY
   CREAM

1. Melt the chocolate with the water in a small saucepan.

2. Add the butter and the vanilla. Stir over gentle heat until the butter is melted.

3. Stir in the cream. Keep warm until ready to serve.

COFFEE SOUFFLÉ WITH CHIPPED CHOCOLATE SAUCE

Nicola Zanghi

4 servings

4 TABLESPOONS (½ STICK) BUTTER
⅔ CUP SUGAR, PLUS 1 TABLESPOON FOR PREPARING THE SOUFFLÉ DISH
1 TEASPOON FINE COCOA
2½ TABLESPOONS INSTANT ESPRESSO COFFEE
PINCH OF CINNAMON

1 CUP MILK
4 TABLESPOONS SIFTED ALL-PURPOSE FLOUR
6 EGG WHITES
PINCH OF SALT
FEW DROPS LEMON JUICE
4 EGG YOLKS
1 TABLESPOON COFFEE LIQUEUR

1. Rub a 1-quart soufflé dish with 1 tablespoon of butter and coat the sides with granulated sugar, then tip out excess sugar.

2. Preheat the oven to 450 F.

3. Dissolve ½ cup sugar, the cocoa, espresso, and cinnamon in the milk over medium heat.

4. In an enameled or stainless-steel 2-quart saucepan, melt the butter over low heat and add the flour. Stir until the flour is "cooked."

5. Whisk the flavored hot milk into the butter and flour and slowly bring it to a boil. Remove the mixture from the heat and transfer it to a large mixing bowl. Allow it to cool for 5 to 10 minutes.

6. Beat the egg whites with salt and lemon juice until they are stiff.

7. Mix the egg yolks into the milk and flour mixture, one yolk at a time. Add the liqueur, then fold in the egg whites in five stages, being careful to work gently. Transfer the mixture to the soufflé dish.

8. Bring a heavy skillet containing water to a boil. Place the skillet in the oven on the floor. Put the soufflé dish in the skillet. Lower the heat to 400 F. and bake for 20 minutes; lower the heat again to 375 F. and bake 25 minutes longer. Be sure that there is always water in the skillet. While the soufflé is baking, make the sauce.

Chipped Chocolate Sauce:
1 PINT HEAVY CREAM
1 TEASPOON VANILLA EXTRACT
2 TABLESPOONS COFFEE LIQUEUR
4 TABLESPOONS SIFTED CONFECTIONERS' SUGAR
⅔ CUP SEMI-SWEET CHOCOLATE, SHAVED

1. Beat the cream until it is almost stiff.

2. Add the vanilla extract, liqueur and sugar and continue to beat a bit more.

3. Transfer the cream to a serving bowl and sprinkle the chocolate over the cream.

THREE ORANGE FLAVORS SOUFFLÉ WITH APRICOT-BLUEBERRY SAUCE (SOUFFLÉ PARFUMS D'ORANGES)

Michael Batterberry

6 servings

As this dessert soufflé contains no thickening agent such as flour or cornstarch, its texture and quality of flavor are like those of a super-aerated dessert omelet. Serve with thick apricot-blueberry sauce on the side. This is more of a purée than a syrupy sauce. It goes particularly well with the orange soufflé—rather like enjoying two desserts at once—as well as with plain, pale cakes.

Apricot-Blueberry Sauce:

1 CUP TIGHTLY-PACKED DRIED APRICOTS (OF THE "TENDERIZED" VARIETY)
1⅔ CUPS WATER
1 4-INCH BROAD STRIP OF ORANGE ZEST
½ CUP SUGAR
3 TABLESPOONS GRAND MARNIER

1½ TABLESPOONS LEMON JUICE
⅓ CUP FRESH ORANGE JUICE
1 TABLESPOON ORANGE-FLOWER WATER
2 CUPS UNSWEETENED BLUEBERRIES, FRESH OR FLASH-FROZEN

1. In an enameled saucepan, bring the apricots, water and the zest to the boil. Stew gently for about 25 minutes.

2. Add the sugar and cook the mixture for 5 minutes longer. Let it cool, then purée it, juices and all, in a blender or food processor along with the Grand Marnier, fruit juices and orange-flower water.

3. Strain the sauce into a serving bowl, cool, and gently stir in the berries, being careful not to crush them.

Soufflé:

4 EGG YOLKS
¾ CUP SUGAR
2 TEASPOONS GRATED ORANGE RIND
2 TABLESPOONS GRAND MARNIER
1 TEASPOON ORANGE-FLOWER WATER (AVAILABLE AT PHARMACIES AND NEAR EASTERN FOOD SHOPS)

PINCH OF SALT
8 EGG WHITES
PINCH OF CREAM OF TARTAR
BUTTER FOR PREPARING SOUFFLÉ DISH AND COLLAR
SUGAR FOR PREPARING SOUFFLÉ DISH AND COLLAR

1. Beat the egg yolks with the sugar until they are thick and lemon-colored.

2. Beat in the orange rind, Grand Marnier, orange-flower water, and the pinch of salt.

3. Beat the egg whites (preferably in a spotless copper bowl) with a large balloon whisk, lifting the egg whites as high as possible to incorporate the maximum amount of air. Add a pinch of cream of tartar and continue beating until the whites are glossy-stiff (as opposed to dry-stiff, their ultimate state if overbeaten).

4. Fold in the yolk mixture as gently as you can with a rubber scraper.

Continued from preceding page

5. Tie a prepared foil collar around a 1½-quart soufflé dish, liberally coated with butter and sprinkled with sugar.

6. Bake in a preheated 425 F. oven for 20 to 25 minutes at most; the soufflé should have a deep golden surface. Serve immediately or even faster!

LEMON SOUFFLÉ WITH MERINGUE TOPPING

Nathalie Dupree

4 servings

You may decide you don't want to add the meringue—it's not essential—but it is easier than it sounds and quite a dashing trick for a festive meal.

BUTTER FOR PREPARING THE SOUFFLÉ DISH
SUGAR FOR PREPARING THE SOUFFLÉ DISH
4 TABLESPOONS (½ STICK) BUTTER
4 TABLESPOONS FLOUR
¾ CUP MILK
5 TABLESPOONS SUGAR

¼ CUP FRESH, STRAINED LEMON JUICE
1 TABLESPOON GRAND MARNIER OR OTHER ORANGE-FLAVORED LIQUEUR
1 TABLESPOON VERY FINELY CHOPPED LEMON PEEL
4 LARGE EGGS, SEPARATED
2 EGG WHITES (EXTRA)

1. Evenly butter a 1-quart soufflé dish. Make a paper collar from a piece of buttered waxed paper long enough to encircle the soufflé dish and to overlap a bit. Fold it in half lengthwise and tie it around the dish with a string.

2. Pour in about 2 tablespoons of sugar. Coat the soufflé dish and the collar with the sugar.

3. Melt the butter in a saucepan. Off the heat, stir in the flour until it is smooth, then add all the milk. Return to the heat. Add the 5 tablespoons of sugar. Bring he mixture to a boil, stirring constantly, until the sauce is smooth and very thick.

4. Remove the pan from the heat and stir in the lemon juice, liqueur and the chopped lemon peel. Add the egg yolks one at a time. The base may wait (covered with plastic wrap so it cannot form a skin) for several hours at room temperature or longer in the refrigerator.

5. Preheat the oven to 400 F. Set the rack in the lower third of the oven. Reheat the lemon sauce lightly—do not boil—to just warm it.

6. Beat the egg whites (preferably in a copper bowl with a balloon whisk) until they are stiff. Mix 2 large spoons of the whites into the warm (not hot) lemon sauce to lighten the mixture. Pour the mixture over the rest of the egg whites. Fold the two together, using a rubber scraper. Do not overfold.

7. Pour the mixture into the sugared dish and smooth the surface with the rubber scraper. Turn down the heat to 375 F. and bake for about 25 to 30 minutes, or

until the soufflé has risen 2 inches above the rim of the dish. While the soufflé is baking, make the meringue.

Meringue:
2 EGG WHITES
⅛ TEASPOON CREAM OF TARTAR
4 TABLESPOONS GRANULATED
   SUGAR

1. Beat the egg whites with the cream of tartar until they are stiff. Add 2 tablespoons of the sugar, and continue to beat until the whites are back to their original stiffness. Add all the rest of the sugar at one time, and fold lightly and quickly. *Do not overfold.* Because of the large amount of sugar added to them, these whites will be different than the whites you folded into the soufflé —heavier and glossier.

2. 5 minutes before the soufflé is done, open the oven door, raise the heat to 450 F. (so the oven temperature will remain constant) and gently slide the rack out halfway. Quickly spread the meringue in decorative swirls on top of the soufflé, and gently, but quickly, slide the rack back into place. Close the oven door and bake the soufflé for 5 to 8 minutes more—until the top of the meringue is lightly browned. Remove the collar and serve the soufflé at once.

FRESH STRAWBERRY SOUFFLÉ

Paula J. Buchholz

6 servings

1 PINT FRESH STRAWBERRIES,
   FINELY CHOPPED (ABOUT 1½
   CUPS)
7 TABLESPOONS SUGAR
1 TABLESPOON GRAND MARNIER
BUTTER FOR PREPARING SOUFFLÉ
   DISH
SUGAR FOR PREPARING SOUFFLÉ
   DISH
3 TABLESPOONS BUTTER
2 TABLESPOONS FLOUR
½ CUP MILK
6 EGG YOLKS
6 EGG WHITES

1. Combine the chopped strawberries, 2 tablespoons of sugar and 1 tablespoon of Grand Marnier. Let them stand about 15 minutes.

2. Butter a 1½-quart soufflé dish or straight-sided mold. Sprinkle it with sugar, tilting the dish to be sure it is thoroughly coated.

3. Melt the 3 tablespoons of butter in a saucepan. Stir in the flour. Continue to cook the mixture for a few minutes, stirring constantly. Gradually add the

Continued from preceding page

milk, continuing to stir until the mixture is thickened and smooth.

4. Remove the pan from the heat and beat in the egg yolks and 3 tablespoons of sugar. Then stir in the strawberries. (This much may be done several hours ahead.)

5. About 30 minutes before serving, beat the egg whites until they are stiff. Fold in the remaining 2 teaspoons of sugar and beat a minute or so longer. Then fold the egg whites into the strawberry mixture.

6. Pour the mixture into the prepared soufflé dish and bake in a 400 F. oven for 20 to 25 minutes. Serve immediately.

BLENDER CHOCOLATE SOUFFLÉ

Carol Cutler

6 servings

½ CUP SUGAR
½ CUP WATER
1 TABLESPOON INSTANT COFFEE
6 OUNCES SEMI-SWEET
  CHOCOLATE
6 EGGS
2 EGG WHITES
½ CUP CREAM
1 TABLESPOON GRAND MARNIER,
  OR OTHER ORANGE LIQUEUR
12 OUNCES CREAM CHEESE
1 TABLESPOON BUTTER

1. In a small pot, melt together the first 4 ingredients (sugar, water, coffee, chocolate). Cool slightly.

2. Break the eggs into the blender and add the egg whites, cream and Grand Marnier. Blend well. With the motor running, scrape the melted chocolate mixture into the blender. Finally add the cream cheese, breaking it into chunks as you add it. When the batter is completely mixed, give a final whirl at high speed.

3. Butter a 1½-quart mold. Pour in the batter to fill the mold three-quarters full. Do not fill to the top. Place in a preheated 375 F. oven and bake for about 45 to 50 minutes for a soufflé that is still moist in the center. The center should be concave; when it is absolutely flat or slightly convex the batter has baked all the way to the center. (I prefer the moist version, spooning some of the liquid in the center as a sauce over the firm portions.) You can test by jiggling the dish; when it is still moist the center will move slightly.

Sweet Cold Soufflés

ICED STRAWBERRY SOUFFLÉ

Emanuel and Madeline Greenberg

8 servings

1 PACKAGE (16 OUNCES) FROZEN
  STRAWBERRY HALVES, THAWED
1 ENVELOPE UNFLAVORED GELATIN
4 EGGS, SEPARATED
6 TABLESPOONS STRAWBERRY
  LIQUEUR
⅓ CUP SUGAR
⅛ TEASPOON SALT
6 LADYFINGERS, SPLIT
2 TABLESPOONS ORANGE LIQUEUR
1 CUP HEAVY CREAM, WHIPPED

1. Drain ½ cup juice from the strawberries; sprinkle the gelatin over the juice to soften.

2. Purée the berries and the remaining juice in a blender or food processor.

3. Combine the egg yolks, strawberry liqueur, sugar and salt in the top of a double boiler. Set over simmering water and beat until thick and creamy. Remove from the heat and cool the mixture to room temperature.

4. Stir the puréed strawberries into the egg yolk mixture and transfer it to a large bowl. Chill, stirring occasionally, until it reaches the consistency of a thick custard sauce.

5. Meanwhile, sprinkle the cut surface of the ladyfingers with the orange liqueur. Arrange them on the bottom and around the sides of a 1½-quart soufflé dish. Tear off a strip of aluminum foil long enough to go around the dish, with a slight overlap. Fold the strip in three, lengthwise, and wrap it around the dish to make a collar that rises 2 inches above the rim. Tie with string to hold it in place.

6. Beat the egg whites until they are stiff, and gently stir about one-quarter of them into the thickened strawberry mixture. Fold in the rest of the whites and then fold in the whipped cream. Pour the mixture into the soufflé dish. Chill until firm, several hours or overnight. Carefully remove the foil collar before serving.

COLD GRENADINE SOUFFLÉ

Julie Dannenbaum

12 servings

2 ENVELOPES PLAIN GELATIN	8 EGG WHITES
½ CUP LEMON JUICE	2 CUPS HEAVY CREAM, WHIPPED
8 EGG YOLKS	1 TABLESPOON VEGETABLE OIL
1 CUP SUGAR	WHIPPED CREAM (OPTIONAL)
1 CUP GRENADINE SYRUP	12 CANDIED VIOLETS (OPTIONAL)

1. In a Pyrex cup, dissolve the gelatin in the lemon juice.

2. Place the cup in a pan of hot water and stir until the gelatin turns clear.

3. Beat the egg yolks with the sugar in a mixer until they are thick and lemon-colored. Add the gelatin mixture and continue to beat until well blended.

4. Pour the mixture into a saucepan and add the grenadine. Cook over medium heat until the mixture thickens slightly, then cool to room temperature.

5. Beat the egg whites until they are stiff, but not dry, and fold them into the cooled mixture.

6. Whip 2 cups of heavy cream until soft peaks form, and gently fold the cream into the mixture.

7. Spoon the mixture into a 1-quart soufflé dish which has been prepared with an oiled collar, or, if you prefer, spoon it into a crystal serving bowl. Chill several hours or overnight.

8. Before serving, gently peel away the oiled collar.

FROZEN MANGO SOUFFLÉ

Florence Fabricant

8 to 10 servings

6 EGGS, SEPARATED AND AT
  ROOM TEMPERATURE
½ CUP FRESH LIME JUICE (2 TO
  2½ LIMES)
1 CUP SUGAR
1½ CUPS FRESH RIPE MANGO,
  PURÉED AND STRAINED (1½ TO
  2 MANGOS)
2 TABLESPOONS LIGHT RUM
1½ CUPS HEAVY CREAM
PINCH OF SALT
PINCH OF NUTMEG

1. Combine the egg yolks and lime juice in the top of a double boiler. Gradually beat in the sugar.

2. Cook over simmering water, stirring slowly, until the mixture thickens enough to coat a metal spoon. This will take a while, approximately 20 minutes. When the mixture has thickened, remove it from the heat and stir in the mango purée and the rum. Allow it to cool at least to room temperature (and preferably cooler) before continuing with the recipe. (You can speed things up by placing the mixture in a metal bowl set in a larger bowl filled with ice and refrigerating it.)

3. While the mango mixture is cooling, affix a high collar to a 1-quart soufflé dish. The collar should extend at least 2 inches above the top of the dish.

4. Whip the cream until it holds its shape, but is not very stiffly peaked. Whip the egg whites with the pinch of salt until stiff, but not dry. Fold the whipped cream and then the egg whites into the cooled mango mixture.

5. Pour the mixture into the prepared soufflé dish, dust with nutmeg and freeze for at least 4 hours. Allow to stand at room temperature for about 15 minutes and remove the collar before serving.

ICED ORANGE-GINGER SOUFFLÉ

Elizabeth Colchie

6 servings

8 LARGE EGG YOLKS
¾ CUP SUGAR
½ CUP ORANGE JUICE
2 TEASPOONS GRATED ORANGE
  RIND
1½ TABLESPOONS (ABOUT 3
  LARGE PIECES) CANDIED GINGER,
  PULVERIZED IN A BLENDER OR
  FOOD PROCESSOR

3 LARGE EGG WHITES
PINCH OF SALT
⅓ CUP HEAVY CREAM

Garnishes:
WHIPPED CREAM, SWEETENED
CANDIED GINGER SLIVERS FOR
  DECORATION

1. With a portable electric mixer (or a rotary beater), beat the yolks and ½ cup of sugar in a bowl until very light and thick; beat in the orange juice.

2. Place the bowl in a pan of simmering water and keep beating until the mixture is very hot, about 130 F., for about 10 minutes. Place the bowl in a larger bowl of ice water and continue beating the mixture until it is cold and forms a ribbon when the beater is lifted; beat in the orange rind and pulverized ginger.

3. Tie a waxed paper or aluminum foil collar around a 1-quart or slightly smaller charlotte mold or soufflé dish. In a bowl, beat the egg whites with a pinch of salt until soft peaks form; gradually add the remaining ¼ cup of sugar and beat until stiff peaks form.

4. In a small bowl, beat the cream until it forms soft peaks.

5. Fold the whites and the cream into the orange mixture with a rubber scraper.

6. Pour the mixture into the prepared mold and chill for at least 6 hours, or overnight. Remove the collar and decorate the soufflé with barely sweetened cream and slivers of candied ginger.

COLD SOUFFLÉ WITH CALVADOS
(SOUFFLÉ GLACÉ AU CALVADOS)

Helen McCully

6 to 8 servings

Custard Base (*crème Anglaise*):
2½ CUPS MILK
1 LARGE PIECE VANILLA BEAN,
  HALVED LENGTHWISE (SEE NOTE
  BELOW), OR 1 TABLESPOON
  PURE VANILLA
8 EGG YOLKS
1 CUP PLUS 3 TABLESPOONS
  SUGAR
1 TABLESPOON ARROWROOT

Italian Meringue:
8 EGG WHITES
PINCH OF SALT
2⅓ CUPS SUGAR
1 CUP WATER

To Finish the Soufflé:
2 CUPS HEAVY CREAM
½ CUP MIXED CANDIED FRUIT,
  DICED FINE
½ CUP CALVADOS

Garnish:
CONFECTIONERS' SUGAR
CANDIED CHERRIES, CUT IN HALF
SLICES OF ANGELICA

1. First, make a collar for a 2-quart soufflé dish. Cut a wide piece of kitchen parchment long enough to go completely around the mold and overlap slightly. Fold the paper over a couple of times. Apply the strip to the outside of the mold, pulling the paper together tightly so that the soufflé mixture cannot run down between the paper and the mold. Secure it with a piece of string, tying it very tightly. Then set it aside.

2. To make the custard base, heat the milk with the vanilla bean or vanilla in a large, heavy enameled saucepan. Combine the egg yolks, sugar and arrowroot in a second heavy saucepan. Beat them with an electric beater until the mixture "makes ribbons." Place the pan on a Flame-Tamer or asbestos mat over low heat, stirring constantly, until warm. Add the hot milk gradually, beating all the while. Continue to cook over low heat until the custard will coat a spoon. Remove from the heat. Cover the pot tightly with plastic wrap and refrigerate.

   Note: If a vanilla bean is used here, the *crème Anglaise* must be strained through a very fine sieve.

3. To make the Italian meringue, place the egg whites in the bowl of an electric mixer. Combine the sugar and water in a saucepan over medium heat and stir until the sugar is dissolved. Boil without stirring until the syrup reaches the soft ball stage (230 F. on a candy thermometer). Beat the egg whites until they begin to hold a shape. Add the syrup in a slow, steady stream, beating constantly. Continue beating until the meringue holds firm, shiny peaks and is cool to the touch.

4. To finish the soufflé, whip the cream until it is stiff but not buttery. Take a very large bowl and combine the *crème Anglaise,* cold meringue, candied fruits, calvados and whipped cream in it, mixing with a rubber scraper. Spoon the mixture into a prepared mold and place in the freezer for several hours or until firm.

5. Just before serving, remove the collar. Sift a light film of confectioners' sugar over the top and garnish with the cherries and angelica.

SOUFFLÉ MONTE CRISTO

Maurice Moore-Betty

6 servings

SALAD OIL FOR COLLAR
6 LARGE EGG YOLKS
½ CUP SUGAR, PLUS 1 TABLESPOON FOR STRAWBERRIES
⅓ CUP WATER
2 ENVELOPES UNFLAVORED GELATIN
⅓ CUP KIRSCH, PLUS 1 TABLESPOON FOR STRAWBERRIES

1½ CUPS HEAVY CREAM
8 LARGE EGG WHITES
3 SQUARES (3 OUNCES) UNSWEETENED CHOCOLATE, GRATED
1 PINT FRESH STRAWBERRIES
SWEETENED WHIPPED CREAM FOR DECORATION

1. Fold a long strip of aluminum foil over lengthwise, and oil it on one side. Tie it around a 1½-quart soufflé dish, oiled side in, to make a collar standing 3 inches above the top.

2. Oil the outside of a tall, straight-sided glass and place it, right side up, in the center of the mold.

3. Beat the egg yolks with ½ cup of sugar until they are thick and lemon-colored.

4. Sprinkle the gelatin over the water and let it stand for 10 minutes; dissolve it over gentle heat, but do not let it boil. Stir it into the egg yolk mixture and then stir in ⅓ cup of kirsch.

5. Whip the cream until it is thick but not stiff, and fold it into the egg yolk mixture.

6. Beat the egg whites until they are stiff, and fold them into the mixture. Pour half the mixture into the prepared soufflé dish, being careful not to get any in the glass, and sprinkle with the grated chocolate.

7. Pour in the remaining soufflé mixture. It shoud rise 3 inches above the rim of the dish. Refrigerate the soufflé for at least 4 hours.

8. Wash the strawberries. Hull them, halve or quarter them if they are large, and sprinkle them with sugar and kirsch to taste.

9. Remove the paper collar from the dish. You may remove the glass by gently running a knife around it and lifting it out, or you may leave it in place. Immediately fill the cavity or glass with strawberries, packing them in tightly and reserving a few for decoration. Garnish the soufflé with rosettes of sweetened whipped cream and strawberries cut in quarters.

EDITORS

Arnold Goldman
Barbara Spiegel
Lyn Stallworth

EDITORIAL ASSISTANT

Christopher Carter

EDITORIAL CONSULTANTS

Wendy Afton Rieder
Kate Slate

CONTRIBUTORS

Introduction by Lyn Stallworth

Michael Batterberry, author of several books on food, art and social history, is also a painter, and is editor and food critic for a number of national magazines. He has taught at James Beard's cooking classes in New York and many of his original recipes have appeared in *House & Garden, House Beautiful* and *Harper's Bazaar.*

Paula J. Buchholz is the regional co-ordinator for the National Culinary Apprenticeship Program. She has been a food writer for the *Detroit Free Press* and for the *San Francisco Examiner.*

Vilma Liacouras Chantiles, author of *The Food of Greece,* writes a food and consumer column for the *Scarsdale* (New York) *Inquirer* and a monthly food column for the *Athenian Magazine* (Athens, Greece).

Ruth Ellen Church, a syndicated wine columnist for the *Chicago Tribune,* had been food editor for that newspaper for more than thirty years when she recently retired. The author of seven cookbooks, her most recent book is *Entertaining with Wine.* Mrs. Church's *Wines and Cheeses of the Midwest* will be published in the fall of 1977.

Elizabeth Colchie is a noted food consultant who has done extensive recipe development and testing as well as research into the history of foods and cookery. She was on the editorial staff of *The Cooks' Catalogue* and has written numerous articles for such magazines as *Gourmet, House & Garden* and *Family Circle.*

Carol Cutler, who has been a food columnist for the *Washington Post,* is a graduate of the Cordon Bleu and L'Ecole des Trois Gourmands in Paris. She is the author of *Haute Cuisine for Your Heart's Delight* and *The Six-Minute Soufflé and Other Culinary Delights.* She has also written for *House & Garden, American Home* and *Harper's Bazaar.*

Julie Dannenbaum is the founding director of the largest nonprofessional cooking school in the country, the Creative Cooking School in Philadelphia. She is the author of *Julie Dannenbaum's Creative Cooking School* and *Menus for All Occasions.* She is also Director of the Gritti Palace Hotel Cooking School in Venice and The Grand Hotel Cooking School in Rome.

Nathalie Dupree has been Director of Rich's Cooking School in Atlanta, Georgia, since it opened in September, 1975. She has an Advanced Certificate from the London Cordon Bleu and has owned restaurants in Spain and Georgia.

Florence Fabricant is a free-lance writer, reporting on restaurants and food for *The New York Times, New York* magazine and other publications. She was on the staff of *The Cooks' Catalogue* and editor of the paperback edition.

Emanuel and Madeline Greenberg co-authored *Whiskey in the Kitchen* and are consultants to the food and beverage industry. Emanuel, a home economist, is a regular contributor to the food columns of *Playboy* magazine.

Diana Kennedy, the leading authority on the food of Mexico, is the author of *The Cuisines of Mexico* and *The Tortilla Book.*

Carole Lalli is a contributing editor to *New West* magazine and its restaurant reviewer. She formerly ran a catering business in New York.

Nan Mabon, a free-lance food writer and cooking teacher in New York City, is also the cook for a private executive dining room on Wall Street. She studied at the Cordon Bleu in London.

Helen McCully is food editor of *House Beautiful* magazine and the author of many books on food, among them *Nobody Ever Tells You These Things About Food and Drink, Cooking with Helen McCully Beside You,* and most recently, *Waste Not, Want Not: A Cookbook of Delicious Foods from Leftovers.* She was a consultant on the staff of *The Cooks' Catalogue.*

Gloria Bley Miller is the author of *Learn Chinese Cooking in Your Own Kitchen* and *The Thousand Recipe Chinese Cookbook.*

Maurice Moore-Betty, owner-operator of The Civilized Art Cooking School, food consultant and restaurateur, is author of *Cooking for Occasions, The Maurice Moore-Betty Cooking School Book of Fine Cooking* and *The Civilized Art of Salad Making.*

Jane Moulton, a food writer for the *Plain Dealer* in Cleveland, took her degree in foods and nutrition. As well as reporting on culinary matters and reviewing food-related books for the *Plain Dealer,* she has worked in recipe development, public relations and catering.

Paul Rubinstein is the author of *Feasts for Two, The Night Before Cookbook* and *Feasts for Twelve (or More).* He is a stockbroker and the son of pianist Artur Rubinstein.

Raymond Sokolov, author of *The Saucier's Apprentice,* is a free-lance writer with a particular interest in food.

Lyn Stallworth was associated with the Time-Life *Foods of the World* series and has written a food column for *Viva* magazine.

Harvey Steiman is food editor of the *Miami Herald.* He has taught cooking classes and lectured on wine and restaurants at the Food and Hotel School of Florida International University.

Joanne Will is food editor of the *Chicago Tribune* and a member of three Chicago wine and food societies.

Paula Wolfert, author of *Mediterranean Cooking* and *Couscous and Other Good Food from Morocco,* is also a cooking teacher and consultant. She has written articles for *Vogue* and other magazines.

Nicola Zanghi is the owner-chef of Restaurant Zanghi in Glen Cove, New York. He started his apprenticeship under his father at the age of thirteen, and is a graduate of two culinary colleges. He is an instructor at the Cordon Bleu school in New York City.